Living the LOVE Chapter

Living the LOVE Chapter

MICHELLE MEDLOCK ADAMS

LION'S HEAD

LIVING THE LOVE CHAPTER
Copyright © 2001 Michelle Medlock Adams

Different versions of some of the stories in this book originally appeared in the *Bedford Times-Mail* newspaper in Bedford, Indiana, *The Believer's Voice of Victory* magazine in Fort Worth, Texas, and *The Standard* magazine in Arlington Heights, Illinois. Special thanks go out to those fine publications and their editorial departments.

All Scripture quotations, unless otherwise indicated, are taken from the *Holy Bible, New International Version*®. NIV®. Copyright © 1973, 1978, 1984 by International Bible Society. Used by permission of Zondervan Publishing House. All rights reserved.

Scripture quotations marked (AMP) are taken from *The Amplified Bible* (AMP). *The Amplified Bible, Old Testament.* Copyright © 1965, 1987 by The Zondervan Corporation. *The Amplified New Testament*, copyright © 1954, 1958, 1987 by The Lockman Foundation. Used by permission.

Scripture quotations marked (NASB) are taken from the *New American Standard Bible*®, © copyright The Lockman Foundation 1960, 1962, 1963, 1968, 1971, 1972, 1973, 1975, 1977. Used by permission.

All rights reserved. No part of this publication may be reproduced, stored in a retrievable system, or transmitted, in any form or by any means electronic, mechanical, photocopying, recording, or otherwise, except for the inclusion of brief quotations in a review, without prior permission in writing from the publishers.

ISBN 1-891668-11-0

Published by Lion's Head Publishing, 3 Coray Court, Little Rock, AR 72223.

Literary development and cover/interior design by Koechel Peterson & Associates, Minneapolis, Minnesota.

Manufactured in the United States of America.

*For my wonderful husband, Jeff.
You make me a better person.*

*In memory of Newell H. Christopher
"Uncle Chris" who always lived the Love Chapter
January 3, 1924–April 2, 2001*

MICHELLE MEDLOCK ADAMS has had a passion for writing since she was a child. While other children scurried outside to play, Michelle curled up under a tree with her notebook and pencil and wrote poetry and short stories. That love for writing continued to grow, and it wasn't long before her writing gained recognition. Now she is a full-time writer, crafting articles for magazines as well as writing women's devotionals, gift books, and children's picture books. She majored in journalism at Indiana University, was an award-winning reporter for the *The Bedford Times-Mail*, and was a full-time feature writer for *The Believer's Voice of Victory* magazine. She resides in Fort Worth, Texas, with her husband, Jeff, and their two daughters, Abby and Allyson.

Love is patient,
love is kind.
It does not envy,
it does not boast,
it is not proud.
It is not rude,
it is not self-seeking,
it is not easily angered,
it keeps no record of wrongs.
Love does not delight in evil
but rejoices with the truth.
It always protects,
always trusts,
always hopes,
always perseveres.
Love never fails.
And now these three
remain: faith, hope and love.
But the greatest of these is love.

(1 CORINTHIANS 13:4-8, 13)

Contents

INTRODUCTION
Learning to Live the Aspects of Love xiii

LOVE IS PATIENT
When It Seems God Is Not Listening 1

LOVE IS KIND
Making a Difference in the World 9

LOVE DOES NOT ENVY
Rejoicing With Others Over Their Successes 17

LOVE DOES NOT BOAST
Sharing God's Blessings Wisely 27

LOVE IS NOT PROUD
Not Being Afraid to Admit You're Wrong 35

LOVE IS NOT RUDE
Looking for Opportunities to Share God's Love 47

LOVE IS NOT SELF-SEEKING
Living for Eternal Purposes 57

LOVE IS NOT EASILY ANGERED
Being Set Free From Hurts 69

LOVE KEEPS NO RECORD OF WRONGS
To Forgive With Grace, Mercy, and Love 79

LOVE DOES NOT DELIGHT IN EVIL BUT REJOICES WITH THE TRUTH
Never Lose Heart When Confronting Darkness 93

LOVE ALWAYS PROTECTS
Living in the Shelter of God's Presence 103

LOVE ALWAYS TRUSTS
Experiencing Peace in the Midst of Adversity 113

LOVE ALWAYS HOPES
Faith Overcomes Against All Odds 121

LOVE ALWAYS PERSEVERES
Never Give Up on the Kingdom of God 129

LOVE NEVER FAILS
Enduring the Storms of Life 145

INTRODUCTION

Learning to Live the Aspects of Love

Last summer as I rushed to make a flight that would take me to a writers' conference in Chicago, I grabbed a magazine at one of the airport newsstands. I didn't reach for *Newsweek*, *Time*, or *Today's Christian Woman* as usual. Instead, I bought *People Weekly* because the front cover caught my eye, "Diet Wars! Celebs Take Sides in the Food Fight."

Wonder how Delta Burke lost so much weight? I thought, looking at her photo as I found my window seat.

Before the plane ever took off, I was lost in the pages of the magazine, learning diet tricks and fitness tips from some of the most beautiful women in Hollywood. Then, when I least expected it, my life was changed forever.

I flipped to an article about two best friends—Esther Kim and Kay Poe. As I began reading their story, my heart pounded with emotion. I could feel the Holy Spirit's presence. "The time had come, as they feared it would, for the two best friends to fight. Esther Kim, 20, and Kay Poe, 18—black belts in taekwondo who are as close as sisters—were each one victory away from claiming the single remaining spot on the U.S. Olympic team heading to Sydney in September. It happened that their final match would be against each other, with one friend destined to win, the other to see her dream die. Those on hand for the Olympic trials in Colorado Springs on May 20 watched as the two combatants—so evenly matched that

Poe won by the narrowest of margins the only other time they'd fought—approached each other on the mat, bowed and turned to the referee, who was to start the bout.

"Instead, before a blow was struck, the referee awarded the match to Poe. Moments earlier he had been told that Esther Kim had forfeited, allowing Poe—who had dislocated her kneecap in a previous fight and could barely stand—to win the women's flyweight championship and make the Olympic team. Kim simply was unwilling to battle her hobbled best friend, even with her own dream so tantalizingly in reach . . .

"Her decision enabled those on hand to witness something more stirring than a fight between two top-level martial artists: They saw an act of selflessness all too rare in pro or amateur sports."*

Tears streamed down my face as I read about this beautiful friendship.

Wow, that's really love in action, I thought.

Just then, I heard the still small voice of the Holy Spirit say, "That's living the Love Chapter, Michelle."

That's when this book was birthed—right there in the airplane at the Dallas/Fort Worth airport. The Lord began showing me people I had encountered in my life who had also lived the Love Chapter. Some I had grown up with. Others I had met over the course of my journalistic endeavors. But all were true examples of God's love. As their stories rolled around in my head, this book took root in my heart. First Corinthians 13 suddenly came alive to me.

I pray that each story touches your heart as it has mine and challenges you to walk in all the aspects of love. I once heard a preacher say, "You may be the only Bible some people ever read." Many people will never go to church or open the Bible for themselves, but they'll

Introduction — Learning to Live the Aspects of Love

watch you—especially if you profess to be a Christian. Secretly, they're searching for answers, and if your love walk isn't where it should be, you may unintentionally turn them away from the real Answer—Jesus Christ.

What a better place this world would be if we all lived the Love Chapter on a daily basis. That's my goal. I hope that after reading this book, it will be yours, too.

NOTES:

*Alex Tresniowski and Gabrielle Cosgriff, "Trading Places," *People Weekly* magazine, June 12, 2000, 99-100.

CHAPTER ONE

LOVE IS PATIENT

When It Seems
God Is
Not Listening

Chapter One ⁓ Love Is Patient

While playing with her six-year-old granddaughter one February morning in 1995, Vera Whitehead of Bedford, Indiana, overheard something on television that caught her attention: "Father/daughter reunions today..."

Vera leaned over and turned up the volume to hear Maury Povich discussing the joyful, long-awaited reunions between daddies and their little girls.

It was something she hadn't thought about in a long time. But as she listened to the incredible stories of those reunions, something began to stir in her heart. And before long, Vera was weeping right along with the daughters as they embraced their long-lost fathers.

I wish I knew where my daddy was, she thought, hugging her granddaughter Andrea to her chest.

Emotions that had been buried for a long time began to surface. After all those years of wondering what had happened to her father, Vera felt a ray of hope. *If it can happen for those women, maybe... maybe it can happen for me,* she thought.

As Vera watched daughters and fathers hug each other with tears of joy after years of separation, she longed to meet her father. She longed to hug him. She longed to tell him that she loved him. She longed to spend time with him, doing all those things she'd never had the chance to do. Her parents had divorced right before she was born, and Vera had never met her father.

The moment the program finished, Vera knew what she had to do. She instinctively dropped to her knees and turned to her heavenly Father in prayer. Andrea knelt beside her. Together, they prayed a simple prayer, asking God to help them find Vera's father. When they had finished, Andrea looked up at her grandma and asked, "Do you think God will answer our prayer?"

Vera wiped her tears and said, "You know, Andrea, I think He will."

THE SEARCH BEGINS

Still feeling quite emotional from what she had just seen on TV, Vera called her cousin Jennifer Turner.

"Did you see the *Maury Povich Show* today?" Vera asked, her voice cracking.

"Yes! I did," Jennifer said, "and I know we're going to find your father."

That same day Vera began her detective work and tracked down the telephone number for a police department in south central Missouri. Vera thought her father might live in that area because he was originally from there; however, no Missouri leads had ever panned out before.

But this time would be different. Somehow she knew God was going to answer her prayer.

Vera called the number and spoke with an officer who referred her to Captain Thorn of the Willow Springs, Missouri, police force. As soon as she hung up the phone, she called Captain Thorn.

"I broke down on the phone," Vera said, remembering. "I wanted him to help me so much. I felt like he was my last shot."

Captain Thorn listened to her story and agreed to help her.

"My wife has just gone through a similar situation," he said. "I understand."

Chapter One — Love Is Patient

FINDING FATHER

Vera figured it would take weeks before she'd hear anything, so she tried not to think about it all the time. When she came home from work the following day, her answering machine was blinking.

Her heart pounded in time with the blinking message.

Could this be it so soon? she thought.

She hit the play button and heard Captain Thorn's voice: "I think I've found the man you're looking for," he said. "Call me."

Vera could hardly believe what she had heard. She replayed the message, took a deep breath, and then picked up the phone and called him.

Captain Thorn explained that he had contacted a man named Gary Malone, a cousin of Vera's she had never met. Gary told Captain Thorn that he thought Vera's father, David Alonzo, lived in Kahoka, Missouri, but that David didn't have a telephone.

Thanking Captain Thorn for all he had done, Vera said goodbye. Then filled with excitement, she quickly called Gary Malone.

"I told Gary how old I was and that I had been trying to find my father, David Alonzo, for a long time," Vera recalled. "He said the man he thought was my father had once mentioned that he had a daughter."

Vera could hardly breathe. She asked Gary questions she had wondered about for years, and he answered all that he could. Then he gave her the telephone number of David Alonzo's neighbor and best friend—Delbert Harper.

Vera immediately called Delbert and shared her story with him, explaining that she'd been searching for her father her entire life.

"Your search is over," Delbert said. "I believe the man you call Daddy lives right next door to me."

THE LONG-AWAITED REUNION

Vera and her husband, Kenny, left for Missouri that Saturday.

"Delbert told me that Daddy was really in shock and not to be surprised if he didn't show much emotion when we came to visit," Vera remembered.

Still, Vera couldn't help but conjure up the perfect reunion in her mind, the kind she'd seen on TV. As they drove along, she reflected on what her life had been like without a daddy. She thought of all those special times when she had wished he had been there to share them with her: birthdays, school functions, holidays, and even the day she got married. Of all those years growing up, she had always dreaded Father's Day. The kids at school had constantly teased her because she didn't know her dad. And now, after forty-two years of waiting patiently, she had finally found him. All those tears of sadness she had shed had now turned into tears of joy.

Could this really be it?

The closer they got to Missouri, the more nervous Vera became. She hoped her father wanted a daughter as much as she wanted a father.

Lord, I know I can trust you. Please help me, she prayed when they finally pulled up in front of the address Delbert Harper had given them.

As Kenny and Vera walked toward the door of Delbert's house, Vera trembled.

I can do this, she thought.

Chapter One ~ Love Is Patient

As soon as she walked through the door, she saw him—her very own daddy. When David saw Vera, he jumped up and threw his arms around her.

"He almost knocked me down," Vera remembered. "He wouldn't let me leave his sight. He kept calling me his daughter over and over again."

After the initial embrace, David told Vera that he had tried to contact her several times when she was a little girl. In fact, he once sent bus tickets to Vera and her mother, but Vera's stepfather had discovered the tickets and tore them up without Vera ever seeing them.

When David didn't hear from Vera or her mother, he just figured they didn't want a relationship with him, so he never tried to contact them again.

"But I always loved you," he told her, patting her hand.

Vera hugged him. "I know, Daddy," she said. "I know."

God had answered Vera's prayers in a miraculous way—even though it took Him forty-two years to do it. "God knew the right time," Vera said. "My grandmother raised me to be patient. She and my grandpa told me about Jesus when I was just a little girl, and I have always trusted in Him even when I didn't understand things in life. I just never gave up."

Today, Vera's father lives with her, and they celebrate Father's Day every day.

Maybe, like Vera Whitehead, you have something that you've been talking to the Lord about for a very long time, and you're frustrated because it seems as though God isn't listening. Maybe your patience is gone and you're ready to give up, but don't quit now.

God has heard every prayer you've ever prayed. He loves you and wants to answer your prayers, but the answer will only come in His timing.

God wants you to wait on His answer with love in your heart because *love is patient*. It may seem as if He has forgotten you, when all along, He has been working on your behalf to bring about the desires of your heart.

FOR FURTHER STUDY: Read Psalm 37:7; Hebrews 6:13-15; James 1:4.

CHAPTER TWO

LOVE IS KIND

*Making a Difference
in the World*

"Sentimentality comes easy.
But caring is hard—it involves doing."
AUTHOR UNKNOWN

Chapter Two — Love Is Kind

Thanks to some bighearted bowlers, several needy Lawrence County, Indiana, families have presents to open every Christmas.

Each year for the past decade, adult and junior bowlers at Brunswick Broadview Bowl in Bedford, Indiana, have opened their hearts and their wallets, raising enough money to adopt several needy families for Christmas. The project is called "Gifts From the Heart," and it's appropriately named. The program got its start at a Bedford Women's Bowling Association meeting.

Members were making small talk, waiting for the meeting to start, when conversation turned to Christmas and all the activities surrounding the upcoming holiday.

"Everybody was talking about how much money they were spending on their children and grandchildren that year," remembered Jeri Cain, a Bowling Association member.

"Isn't it a shame that some kids don't get any presents?" someone said.

"It's sad," another chimed in, "but there's nothing we can do."

Jeri thought about it for a moment and then asked, "Why not? Why can't we do something to help? Why can't we find families who need help and buy them gifts?"

No one had any instant answers, but they all had big hearts. And the more they talked about it, ideas started to come as more and more people said they wanted to help in any way possible. Thus, "Christmas From the Heart" was born.

That first year the program was a whirlwind experience. In just ten days, Jeri and bowling buddy Marilyn Heady were able to raise $800. With the help from some local agencies, they found two needy families they could bless that Christmas season. They went out and purchased gifts, wrapped them, and delivered the presents to the families' homes.

"We worked fast," Marilyn said, grinning.

Since that first year, donations for the "Christmas From the Heart" program have grown. The second year, more than $1,000 were donated for the project, and the giving has continued to increase each year.

"The adult league bowlers make the project happen each year," Jeri said. "Everyone is so willing to give so others can enjoy Christmas. Even the junior bowlers do their part. They bring in canned goods to distribute to the needy families."

In addition to the canned goods, the bowlers also purchase seven or eight bags of groceries for each family. And if the selected family has a special Christmas dinner request, Jeri and Marilyn make it a point to buy those specific food items to make those dinner wishes a reality.

"We'll buy beautiful Christmas hams or whatever they want. We want to make it as individual and personal as we can," Jeri said.

That's why the bowlers call it "adopting" families for the holidays. They really do take care of each family during the Yuletide season from beginning to end. That even includes buying a Christmas tree and decorations if those Christmas basics are needed.

"We took a tree with all the trimmings to one home, and this three-year-old little girl got so excited when she saw it," Jeri recalled. "She said, 'Oh, Mommy, can we keep it?' They'd never had a Christmas tree before."

Chapter Two ～ Love Is Kind

The following Christmas, that thankful mother telephoned Jeri and asked her to stop by over the holidays. When Jeri walked into the woman's home, a big smile spread across her face. In their living room stood a big, beautiful artificial tree that the woman's church had given the family. And it was trimmed with all the decorations the bowlers had donated the previous year.

"She was so proud of it," Jeri said. "I was so happy for her."

From tree trimmings to toys, the bowlers make sure each family has a joyous Christmas. They go all out to make the holiday a memorable time.

"We make sure each person receives gifts," Marilyn said. "Even the parents. It's important for the children to see them included as well."

When Jeri and Marilyn receive the families' wish lists, they try their best to fill each member's request.

"We want to get that child what he or she really has their heart set on," Jeri said. "As much money that is given each year, there's no excuse why every single child shouldn't be able to get up on Christmas morning and have something special under the tree to open up."

Other philanthropic groups sometimes overlook the older children. Not the bowlers. They buy presents for children of all ages.

"Kids twelve to eighteen still need presents," Jeri said. "Those kids need jeans, hats, and shoes, too."

Over the years, microphones, hair bows, blue jeans, Barbie dolls, crayons, CDs, and even vacuum cleaners have been wrapped up for families. And there are two gifts that every family receives—a disposable camera and a book of Bible stories.

"We mark the camera, 'Open me first,' so they can capture their special Christmas memories on film," Jeri explained. "And the book of Bible stories is so they can explain to their children what Christmas is really all about. We want them to hear the real Christmas story—of how God gave His Son, Jesus, to save the world."

One year the benevolent bowlers delivered presents to a family whose house had dirt floors. The children happened to be home, and Jeri didn't want to spoil the surprise. Wearing her red Santa hat, she pretended to be Santa's head elf.

"I told the little boy that Santa sent me to deliver the presents because he was so busy," she recalled. "He looked up at me with big eyes and said, 'Really? These presents are for me?'"

That little boy isn't the only recipient who's been surprised by the bowlers' goodwill over the years. One woman asked Jeri why the bowlers would help a perfect stranger. "Why would anyone care if my kids have Christmas or not?" she asked.

Jeri just smiled and said, "Because this is what Christmas is all about."

"To me, this is Christmas," Jeri added. "I just wish we could do more. For every family we help, I'm sure there are twelve more out there who need assistance."

The bowlers in Bedford aren't giving to be recognized. They've simply found that giving from their hearts and wallets each year is even more gratifying than getting three strikes in a row.

"I can't stand the thought of parents having to tell their kids that Santa lost the directions to their house again this year. Every child deserves a merry Christmas. We're just glad we can help."

There are people like these Bedford bowlers all over the world, making a difference one family at a time. Many well-doers may

Chapter Two ~ Love Is Kind

never get any earthly recognition for their kind acts, but God will honor them someday.

Why? Because their motive is love, and love is kind.

Whether it's giving up your subway seat to an elderly person or offering to watch a single mother's children while she goes to the doctor—small acts of kindness are not small in God's eyes. And they do not go unnoticed by Him either!

We find that out in Matthew 25, verses 31-46. Let's look at how God views the acts of kindness we do for others.

> *When the Son of Man comes in his glory, and all the angels with him, he will sit on his throne in heavenly glory. All the nations will be gathered before him, and he will separate the people one from another as a shepherd separates the sheep from the goats. He will put the sheep on his right and the goats on his left.*
>
> *Then the King will say to those on his right, "Come, you who are blessed by my Father; take your inheritance, the kingdom prepared for you since the creation of the world. For I was hungry and you gave me something to eat, I was thirsty and you gave me something to drink, I was a stranger and you invited me in, I needed clothes and you clothed me, I was sick and you looked after me, I was in prison and you came to visit me."*
>
> *Then the righteous will answer him, "Lord, when did we see you hungry and feed you, or thirsty and give you something to drink? When did we see you a stranger and invite you in, or needing clothes and clothe you? When did we see you sick or in prison and go to visit you?"*
>
> *The King will reply, "I tell you the truth, whatever you did for one of the least of these brothers of mine, you did for me."*

The Bible also instructs us in Romans 12:13 to, "Share with God's people who are in need." And in James 2:8, it says, "Love your neighbor as yourself, you are doing right."

So no matter how small your act of kindness is in the world's eyes, just know that it's enormous in the Father's eyes.

Kindness motivated by love can break down barriers, restore hope, repair hurting hearts, encourage the downhearted, bring unity to divided families, and inspire others to act in kindness, too.

Keep living the verse, "Love is kind," and watch your world change around you.

FOR FURTHER STUDY: Read Proverbs 14:31; 18:16; 19:17; Mark 12:41-44; Acts 4:32-35.

CHAPTER THREE

LOVE DOES NOT ENVY

*Rejoicing With Others
Over Their Successes*

Chapter Three ⸺ Love Does Not Envy

It was Christmas 1962, and Elvis was King. The Beatles ruled the airwaves, and Stepp Stevens and his brother, Rick, were training to be the next famous rockers. At ages four and five, the brothers spent much of their time singing and dancing in front of the television, pretending to be their rock-and-roll heroes.

But that day the boys had something else to be excited about—presents! They ripped open their gifts one by one, showing each other the cool stuff that Santa had brought them. Then, it happened. Rick unwrapped the ultimate Christmas gift—a glorious guitar. Stepp quickly searched through the rest of his packages, ripping them open in great anticipation of getting his very own guitar. Finally, there were no more presents to open, and Stepp was guitarless.

"Where's my guitar?" Stepp cried out in tears.

There was no answer. Santa had really messed up.

"All I could think about was . . . Rick had a guitar and I didn't," Stepp remembered. "That really bothered me."

One day when Rick was gone, Stepp picked up that guitar, stared at it a moment, and then put his foot right through the back of it. Not even Elvis could have revived that mangled musical instrument.

As Stepp walked away from the crushed guitar, he felt justified in what he'd done.

"If I couldn't have a guitar," Stepp said, "I didn't think Rick should have one either."

FOLLOWING THE DREAM

Twenty years later, Stepp was in the midst of pursuing his musical dreams. He had been writing songs and playing his own guitar since age sixteen, but it wasn't until 1984 that Stepp was in the studio recording his very first Christian music project. He found every part of the process fascinating and exciting.

"I had the best producer and musicians working on my music," Stepp said. "I figured I was on my way."

Before long Stepp was on the road sharing the love of Jesus Christ through his music. After all those years of dreaming, it had finally become a reality. Now that he had become a professional artist, Stepp was encouraged to join an Artists Bible Study that met regularly in Dallas, Texas. The study was taught by one of the industry's top producers and recording artists.

"If you were anybody in the music business, you went to this spiritual gathering," Stepp explained. "I just knew that I was going to be blessed and taken to a new spiritual level by attending that Bible study.

"I thought that hanging out, shoulder to shoulder, with some of my music heroes was going to mature my faith."

Stepp walked into that first Bible study with great hopes and expectations. The worship service was grand, ushering in the very presence of Christ. After a while, the leader came forward and gave a dynamic message, which deeply inspired Stepp. When the study ended, he mingled with the other attendees, talking with them about their newest hit songs. The room was full of the "who's who" in the Christian music world.

As Stepp introduced himself to many of the top artists, session

Chapter Three ~ Love Does Not Envy

musicians, producers, writers, and "wanna-be's," something started happening inside of him.

The night continued, and Stepp listened to story after story of musical success from one artist after another. It seemed that everyone had a more successful career than Stepp was experiencing. And with each success story he heard, Stepp began to feel worse about his own musical career, which seemed to be going nowhere.

"I walked away from that Bible study feeling terrible," he admitted. "In fact, I was downright miserable. Everyone had more success than I did. Even the other wanna-be's had songs on the radio, record deals happening or about to happen, and full concert schedules with waiting lists. It seemed as though I was the only one who wasn't 'in' or 'happenin'."

Stepp tried hard to be happy for his peers, smiling at everyone while secretly wishing he could smash the guitars of every well-known Christian artist in the room.

"My attitude was terrible," he said. "I began hating myself. I even began hating God for not blessing me with the same success."

On the drive home that night, Stepp continued to compare himself with everyone else's fame and success. Soon he spiraled down into self-pity and envy. He decided he didn't like the way he looked. He didn't like his new project he was working on. Nobody was paying him enough money. He didn't like the way he played guitar, and he thought all of his songs were nothing but trash. In fact, he decided that, all in all, his whole life wasn't worth much of anything.

"At one point, I even began contemplating suicide. I didn't think life was worth living anymore," Stepp shared. "The only thing I was thankful for was that I'd found out in time that I was a low-life, unsuccessful artist before I went forward and proved what an idiot I really was."

THE REVELATION

Stepp stumbled around in depression for days, grumbling about everything. After several weeks of feeling sorry for himself, he was forced to pull it together to perform at a concert he'd already committed to do.

It certainly wasn't a big venue. There were no television cameras. No record producers in the audience scouting for new artists. No deluxe sound system or elaborate light show. Nope, this was a concert in west Texas in the middle of a dust hole. It was a Christian camp for high-school kids. There were about 350 campers in all.

Still, it was a gig. Once Stepp began to sing, he put his heart into every song. He sang as if there were 350,000 people in the audience. He forgot about what he had been going through and ministered to those kids through music with everything he had.

"During that concert, many of those kids found new hope in a God who loved them," Stepp remembered. "I knew it had been a good concert."

But Stepp couldn't understand why the teens weren't buying any of his tapes, CDs, or T-shirts. He asked the program director.

"Stepp, most of these kids come from single-parent homes," the director answered. "Many are on food stamps. Some of them were only able to attend camp because of scholarships that were offered."

When Stepp heard that, his heart broke for those kids, and he couldn't stop thinking about it the rest of the night.

The next morning, Stepp went to the camp director and asked him to make a special announcement: "Any camper who wanted a

Chapter Three ~ Love Does Not Envy

Stepp Stevens tape, T-shirt, or CD can have one for free."

The campers swarmed the product table, snatching up the treasured tapes and T-shirts.

"It looked like somebody had just announced that free money was available," Stepp said. "That was the happiest moment in my life. I ran out of tapes and T-shirts. I left with an empty box but a full heart. I thanked God for the kids, the opportunity, my songs, my message, my ministry, and my life. I couldn't wait until the next Artists Bible Study to tell everyone what had happened."

The following week Stepp attended the Bible study, anxious to share his good news. Once again, the singing was great. The message was incredible, and Stepp was pumped. But during the fellowship time, that familiar green-eyed monster of envy reared its ugly head. Within thirty minutes, Stepp hated his ministry and his life again.

Driving home, he began reflecting on everything.

Why do I feel so useful when I'm ministering, but so insignificant when I'm around my peers? he wondered.

Just then, he felt the Holy Spirit's presence.

"You just learned the difference between the power of love and the power of envy," the Holy Spirit gently spoke into his spirit.

Suddenly, it all seemed so clear.

"At the Bible study, the main goal of most people was self-promotion. It was like a cattle call to move forward and be branded 'successful' with everybody's words of praise and even more lucrative contracts. You weren't somebody unless you could prove how much talent you had and how much the industry needed you," Stepp said. "As I heard local and major artists share about their accomplishments over and over again, I began trying to match them. When I didn't measure up, I chose envy.

"Soon my envy caused me to lose sight of what God had already given me. Envy destroyed my God-given self-image and self-esteem. Envy clouded my vision. Envy turned my successes and accomplished goals into worthless trash. Envy changed my world from a blue of opportunity to the darkness of greed. I couldn't even hear God's voice because I was too busy wanting what others had. I was counting their blessings and discounting mine. I was lost in self-pity, fear, anxiety, intense jealousy, greed, resentment, spite, and desire."

Envy almost destroyed him, but love rescued him.

"God taught me to lose myself and build up others," Stepp shared. "When I was singing at the camp concert, my focus was those kids and the message that God had for them. I knew I was a conduit of God's love, assigned to that place and time. I had a job to do. It wasn't about me and my needs. It was all about them and God's special plan for their lives. As I learned the truth of that, a new joy and happiness flowed all over me. Why? Because love does not envy."

THE LOVE GOES ON

Stepp returned to the Artists Bible Study, but this time he was ready and armed with God's love. He checked envy at the door.

"This time I knew who I was and what my calling and purpose were," Stepp said. "I knew what had caused me to hate all that God had given me. This time the tables were turned. I set my goal to mentor and not manipulate. I encouraged and restored hope to those I spoke with. I found out what was happening in their lives and encouraged them to pursue their goals and achieve them."

When he got into his car that night, Stepp had to smile. He had found the secret—when envy shows up, there are serious side effects. But when love shows up, there are many benefits.

Chapter Three ~ Love Does Not Envy

Later that week, Stepp received a call from a well-known artist, asking if he would speak at the next Artists Bible Study. Stepp gladly accepted. God had taught him a love lesson, and now he had the opportunity to share that lesson with all of his peers and mentors. And that's exactly what he did.

Today, some of those same artists whom Stepp envied are his very best friends.

"I don't attend that Bible study anymore, but I learned a great lesson there," Stepp shared. "I made a decision that my success was going to be built upon love.

"I never did make it to the top of the music charts," Stepp said, "but I made it to the top of many hearts, and that's enough reward for me."

Envy is a tough one. It creeps into our lives without us even knowing it and takes residence unless we force it out with love. Are you experiencing envy in your life? Can you relate to Stepp's story in any way? Maybe you're in an industry or a career that is highly competitive and it's hard to live free of envy. I understand. I've been there. But let me tell you what I've discovered. Until you can rejoice with others over their accomplishments and breakthroughs, you'll never reach your own goals and live out your own dreams.

God can't promote you and reward you if you're walking in envy. The Bible says that where envy and strife dwell, there also dwells every other kind of evil. How can God promote evil? He can't. We tie His hands with our envy and jealousy and prevent Him from sending the blessings He has for us. So what's the solution? Confess your envious heart to the Lord right now. Admit that you've been envious of your buddy who got the promotion over you. Admit that you've been envious of your best friend ever since she inherited that huge sum of money. God already knows anyway. But if you confess it before Him, He can cleanse you and take that envy away and replace it with His glorious love. Then you won't have to force a smile when others succeed around you. You can be truly happy for them, knowing that your breakthrough is just around the corner.

God's got enough success and blessings for every single one of us, and He can't wait to see you walking in your dreams. So the next time you're challenged in this area, think of Stepp's story. Once he gave his envy to God, the Lord was able to use him in mighty ways. Today, he runs two successful businesses, has a lovely wife and children, and uses his music to heal hurting hearts whenever the Lord directs. Envy is the destroyer, but love is the restorer. Give your envy to God and watch Him work in your life.

FOR FURTHER STUDY: Read Psalm 37:1-3; Proverbs 14:30; 27:4; 1 Corinthians 3:3-4; James 3:16.

CHAPTER FOUR

LOVE DOES NOT BOAST

*Sharing God's
Blessings Wisely*

Chapter Four ~ Love Does Not Boast

Ray Lacelle and Jim Miller (not his real name) were great friends. Whether just kicking back talking sports or engaging in deep conversation about God, their friendship was an easy one. They had been buddies for a long time.

"We had both been raised in similar traditional church environments, so we understood a lot about each other," Ray shared.

God had led both of them separately to the same large nondenominational church in the Dallas, Texas, area. There they were learning about faith, how to daily walk with God, and how to share what they'd learned with others.

"We had always had an awareness of the gospel," Ray explained, "but we were just coming into a deeper personal, daily relationship with God."

They soon realized that their deeper spiritual walks were leading them down different career paths. Formerly, Ray was a professional actor/model, and Jim was a salesman, but both felt called to the ministry.

"That church really affected us at that time in our lives," Ray observed. "Before long, both of us desired to serve the Lord in ministry, and did so there, because it had influenced each of us in such a dramatic way."

At first Ray and Jim worked the telephone lines, and Jim's wife, Peg, worked as a secretary in the ministry. Ray's and Jim's jobs were entry-level positions, but they didn't care. They were just happy to be serving God and taking His Word to those who desperately needed it.

Because of their solid work ethic and diligence, it wasn't long before both men were promoted. Ray began working in communications, and Jim became the trusted ministry shuttle service. His duties were to take visiting ministers and dignitaries to and from the airport.

"To the world, it was a taxi driver position," Ray said, "but to the ministry, this was a very important position. It was an honor."

Jim worked crazy hours—seventy hours a week sometimes—transporting people at all hours of the day and night. Sometimes it was a thankless job, and it didn't pay much, but Jim was happy to serve in that capacity.

Then something wonderful happened.

Jim and Peg were blessed with a great deal of money from a completely unexpected source—more money than either of them had seen their whole lives. It was as if heaven had opened up its windows and poured down unspeakable blessings upon Jim and Peg.

Within just a few weeks, they had a brand-new Lexus 400 series and a beautiful new five-bedroom home in an exclusive North Dallas neighborhood. One minute they were working-class folk, struggling to make a living, and the next minute they were thirty-somethings who were financially set! Jim and Peg could hardly believe their good fortune. They rejoiced together, making plans and dreaming dreams they hadn't dare dream before. It was like a fairytale.

Still, Jim kept his job at the ministry, working just as hard if not harder than he had before. He knew God had called him to minister in whatever capacity he could, and that calling hadn't changed just because he'd come into some money.

"Before he got this financial breakthrough, they were living in a small apartment and driving a seven-year-old Honda Accord," Ray

Chapter Four — Love Does Not Boast

said. "They weren't into material things. In fact, like myself, they had set aside their career aspirations in order to serve the Lord in His work."

VOCAL AND SILENT TESTIMONIES

For weeks Jim continued driving the old Honda Accord to work, worried he might offend someone with his extravagant new vehicle. Finally, he felt that he should tell Ray. After all, they shared almost everything together. So he called his friend.

"Ray, Peggy and I want to share something with you, but I don't know how to tell you," Jim said.

"What is it?" Ray asked.

"I want to show you this blessing that God has given us," Jim shared. "I want you to enjoy our new car with us."

In just a few minutes, Jim and Peg picked up Ray, and they went for a ride in the beautiful luxury sedan.

"It even had a telephone in its steering wheel," Ray remembered. "Nobody had a phone in the steering wheel back then. It was an amazing car."

Together, the three friends praised God, laughing and celebrating His goodness.

"It was awesome," Ray said.

But Jim's reaction to his financial miracle was even more awesome to Ray.

Jim didn't quit his job. He continued serving the ministry with his whole heart. Jim didn't tell his financial miracle to the rest of the staff. He only told a select few. In fact, he didn't do anything that most people do when they come into a lot of money.

"In the world when someone suddenly wins, or is somehow blessed with a large sum of money, they often quit their jobs and shout their good fortune from the rooftops," Ray said. "But Jim didn't. His heart was so pure and his response so mature. Not one time did I ever see him act irresponsible, haughty, or presumptuous about his financial breakthrough. It was one of the most authentic demonstrations of humility that I'd ever seen. He only shared his good news with those he felt would be blessed by it."

One day as Ray and Jim were discussing Jim's monetary blessing, Ray asked him why he hadn't told more people about his newfound wealth.

"I don't want to cause anybody to stumble with jealousy or envy," Jim said. "I want to share my testimony of God's goodness, but only with the people that God directs me to tell. If their hearts aren't ready to receive what I have to say, my story might hurt them."

Jim's humble and wise response so impressed Ray that he's never forgotten it.

"I learned a lot from my friend," Ray said. "Others might say that he should have broadcast his financial miracle, but I understand why he didn't. I learned that there is a time and a season for everything. There is a time to keep our testimony quiet and a time to shout it from the rooftops. We have to be sensitive enough to know that our testimony may not be a blessing to someone at that moment because we don't know what that person is going through.

"For some, hearing Jim's testimony would've brought hope knowing that God is no respecter of persons—if He did it for one, He could do it for another. But the same testimony could have caused great discouragement for somebody else. The key is this: We have to listen to that still small voice and endeavor to follow the Holy Spirit's leading.

"The Bible says not to do anything that would cause your

Chapter Four ~ Love Does Not Boast

brother or sister to stumble. We should never allow our liberty to be a stumbling block for anyone else. Sometimes it's best not to share anything at all and just let our light shine."

That's what Jim continues to do.

Today, he and Peg have two precious children, and he has gone back to school. They've moved out of that big luxurious house north of town and into an apartment near campus. Jim is enrolled in a denominational seminary to further his education so that he can better influence people with the love of God. And Ray also continues serving the Lord in the Dallas/Fort Worth metroplex. He heads up a nonprofit organization, ministering in churches as well as conducting seminars that teach biblical principles through a servant-minded perspective to professionals and the underprivileged.

"I believe that God's Word teaches us to be givers of grace and goodness wherever we go. His desire for us to prosper is so we can tell of and demonstrate His love for every individual. That must be our motivation for receiving, giving, and telling of God's goodness in our lives.

"I praise God that I was allowed to see early in my Christian life a demonstration of true humility and a concern for others more than for one's self," Ray shared. "It has forever changed me."

Sometimes boasting is nothing more than just getting carried away. We've all done it. When something exciting happens in our lives, it's only natural to want to share every detail of our success with those around us. And that's not necessarily a bad thing. It is something we need to be conscious of in our love walk.

As Ray pointed out, sometimes we can be overly boastful about our blessings. Instead of just bragging on Jesus, we step out of the land of testifying and into Boastville, USA. It's easy to do. I've done it myself.

While writing the annual Christmas cards last year, I shared about the kids, my husband's job, and my recent book sales. I wrote: "Abby and Ally are making straight A's, hallelujah! Jeff is doing really well in his career; and I am soon to be published—praise the Lord!" I went on and on, sharing every detail of God's goodness in each situation. It was an attempt to update our friends on what had transpired over the last twelve months, but in the process I became Betty Bragger. My heart was right, but my words were wrong.

A month later, I saw a good friend of mine who said, "Wow, I read your Christmas card and thought, 'What am I doing with my life?'"

Oh no! What have I done? I cringed. *I've hurt her and discouraged her.* Of course that wasn't my intent, but my words weren't uplifting to her. They had caused the opposite effect. We spoke for a few more minutes and hugged before we went our separate ways, but my heart hurt knowing that I had come off so boastful. Suddenly I wished I could retrieve every card I'd written. After all, Christmas is all about Jesus, not about my family and our triumphs.

Since that day, I've been very watchful over my words. Like Ray, I've learned something very important from my friend. There is a time to share your blessings, and there's a time to be still. Knowing the difference only comes with spiritual maturity. I am still attaining in that area of my love walk, but God knows my heart. He knows your heart, too. If you struggle in this area, ask God to help you be sensitive to His voice so that you'll know when to shout your blessings and when to let your light shine quietly.

FOR FURTHER STUDY: Read Deuteronomy 8:18; Proverbs 11:2; Jeremiah 13:15; Ephesians 4:1-2, 29.

CHAPTER FIVE

LOVE IS NOT PROUD

*Not Being Afraid
to Admit
You're Wrong*

Chapter Five — Love Is Not Proud

"Martha, did you pack my blue pants?" Ed Dorsey called to his wife in the other room.

"Yes," she answered.

The Dorseys had enjoyed many long weekends in Chicago during their forty-two years of marriage. Chicago had such an international flavor to it—quite different from their hometown of Anderson, Indiana.

Ed was looking forward to another enjoyable weekend, but as he walked into the other room to find Martha, pain shot through his lower back.

It must be my sciatic nerve, he thought. *I better get some pain pills for the trip, or I won't be much company for Martha.*

BAD NEWS

While Martha finished packing, Ed headed to the local medical clinic.

"Where does the pain begin?" asked the doctor.

"Right around my tailbone area," Ed answered. "I think it's my sciatic nerve. My wife and I are leaving for Chicago this afternoon, and I was hoping I could get some pain pills for the trip."

The doctor nodded, still pushing Ed's lower back to determine if the pain was muscular or something else.

"Mr. Dorsey," the doctor said, "I want to do a prostate exam."

After a brief examination, the doctor sat down with Ed and explained that a normal prostate is about the size of a chestnut and very soft.

"But yours," he said, "is as large as an orange and as hard as a tabletop. That's not good. I'm afraid you can't go to Chicago. You need to see a urologist right away."

Ed went to a urologist early the next morning, and it was confirmed that his prostate was abnormal. The urologist then administered a Prostate Specific Antigen (PSA) test to see if a biopsy would be necessary.

A retired Baptist preacher, Ed knew what to do. He and Martha turned to God, putting the situation in His hands. Two days later, Ed was called in to discuss the test results.

"The test is considered normal if you score four or less," the doctor explained. "Ninety-nine percent of all malignancies are found between five and twenty-five."

"What was mine?" Ed asked anxiously, hoping to avoid a biopsy.

"One thousand and ninety-four."

Ed could hardly breathe.

"I've only had twelve patients with a count that high in my thirty years of practicing medicine," the doctor said.

"And," Ed whispered, "what happened to those people?"

"I hate to tell you this," the doctor said, pausing, "but they all died very soon. I'm so sorry."

A biopsy later concluded what they already knew—Ed had Stage D prostate cancer, meaning the cancer had already spread into his upper body and bones. He was scheduled for immediate chemotherapy and radiation treatments.

During Ed's first oncology visit, the doctor explained about upcoming treatments and possible side effects, but Ed only wanted to know one thing: "How long do I have?"

"Nobody really knows," the doctor answered.

Chapter Five ～ Love Is Not Proud

"Listen, I am not a little boy," Ed said. "I want to know my odds."

"You may have two or three days, two or three weeks, or at the most, two or three months."

Ed stumbled out of the office and into his car, collapsing over the steering wheel in tears. In a matter of a few days, his entire world had come crumbling down all around him.

How will I tell Martha? he thought.

When he arrived home, Martha met him at the door. The look on his face said it all.

She knew.

"When I told her," Ed reflected, "I've never seen such pain in anyone's eyes. Martha was crushed, and I was crushed. We love each other very dearly, and we couldn't bear the thought of being apart.

"It wasn't that I was afraid of dying. I knew I'd go to heaven. I just wasn't prepared to leave my family—my wife, my two children, and my three grandchildren."

Ed began chemotherapy and radiation in June 1997. He lived a week, beating the two-or-three-day mark. Then he lived a month, passing the two-or-three-week hurdle. Finally, he made it to the fourth month, outliving the most optimistic three-month prognosis, but Ed grew weaker with each day. And the pain intensified so much that he could no longer sleep for more than an hour or two at night.

Martha prayed that God would heal him. Their children, son-in-law, and grandchildren prayed, and so did their church friends. They believed it was possible for God to heal him.

But Ed didn't believe himself that he could be healed.

In seminary he had been taught that miracle healings had ceased long ago. He believed there had been isolated miraculous healings throughout history, but that healings today took place only at the hands of doctors.

"I didn't know anything about miraculous healing," Ed explained. "What little I had heard about healing had been criticized and sometimes even ridiculed."

Ed faced what future that remained with much fear and little hope.

A THANKSGIVING MIRACLE

When Thanksgiving came, Ed was truly thankful—thankful to still be alive and spending another holiday with his family. Dinner was served with all the fixings, but no one seemed very hungry. A dark cloud hung over all the festivities.

"You didn't have to be a brilliant physician to know that I was dying," Ed said, remembering. "They all knew it. It was only a matter of time."

After dinner the family watched a movie, and then they began the Dorsey family ritual—decorating the house for Christmas. They put up the Christmas tree, wrapped a few presents, and placed poinsettias throughout the home before calling it a day. As the last of the children left, Martha helped Ed into his easy chair near the fireplace and gave him a kiss before retiring for the night.

Ed tried to sleep, but the pain was too great. Hour after hour, he stared at the brightly wrapped Christmas presents, wondering if he would live long enough to unwrap any of them. At 3:30 in the morning, as the fire died down, Ed watched the last embers flickering among the ashes, and he began to cry. Falling onto the floor in front of his chair, he cried out to God, "Spare me, Lord! Please spare me! Just let me live a little longer with my family."

Chapter Five ~ Love Is Not Proud

Several minutes went by before Ed got up and sat back in his easy chair. It wasn't until he was already sitting that he realized how easily he had been able to stand up and sit down. Instinctively, Ed reached his arms around to his lower back and pushed on it.

It didn't hurt!

He couldn't believe it. For the first time in months, there was no pain!

"I didn't see anything. I didn't hear anything. And no angel, apostolic healer, or doctor was there. I was alone with God," Ed explained. "I didn't feel any heat shoot through my body as some people do. I just got healed."

Ed stood and walked up the stairs into the guestroom so he wouldn't disturb Martha, and he slept for nine hours straight. The next morning, Ed breezed into the kitchen.

"My! You are better!" Martha said.

Ed just smiled and nodded. He was afraid to share the details of what had happened the night before because he wasn't exactly sure what had occurred. Finally, after a few days, Ed told Martha everything. He wondered if she thought he was crazy. They decided to tell no one except their family.

GOD'S SPONTANEOUS REMISSION

About two weeks later, Ed was scheduled for another PSA test. As always, when the results came back, Ed returned to discuss them with the doctor. This time Ed was the doctor's last appointment before Christmas.

"The doctor looked at me kind of strange," Ed remembered. "He just stared at me, so I asked him what was wrong."

He said nothing.

"Is my PSA higher than before?" Ed urged.

"No," the doctor said. "It's only 3.1. It has dropped 1,091 points."

Ed smiled.

"But I doubt it is accurate," the doctor continued. "We'll have to do another test. The lab has obviously messed up. I'm going to use a private lab this time. I'll call you after the holidays."

Ed left the office rejoicing. He couldn't stop smiling. Now he had medical confirmation—something miraculous had taken place that November night in his living room. He didn't know what, but he knew Who.

Christmas 1997 was very special. As Ed opened his presents, he remembered that November night when he had stared at those same gifts and wondered if he would live long enough to open them.

Ed met with his doctor in early 1998 to learn what the most recent PSA test had revealed.

"This is unusual . . . if not impossible," the doctor told Ed. "I can't explain it, but your score is less than 1 percent. It's 0.1, in fact. I don't understand. We'll just watch it."

Ed didn't understand either. He just knew that something wonderful had happened to him, something supernatural. Several months went by, and Ed continued feeling great. Still, he and Martha hadn't told anyone about Ed's recovery because of their own confusion.

Later that year, Ed was scheduled for a routine physical exam with his longtime family doctor, a retired medical missionary.

After the examination, Ed sat across from his physician, awaiting the diagnosis. The doctor held Ed's original PSA test score in one hand and his last test scores in the other, studying them for several minutes. Finally, he looked up and asked, "Ed, can you explain

Chapter Five ～ Love Is Not Proud

to me how the tests were so bad here and so good here?"

Should I tell him? Ed thought.

Feeling the Holy Spirit's prompting, Ed shared his testimony of that miraculous night.

"I've never really believed in miraculous healings," Ed told the doctor, "but all I know is that I have been better since that night."

The doctor looked thoughtfully at Ed and said, "Don't you know that there are times when doctors don't know what to do, and then God comes and touches the sore spot? And, Ed, He has come and touched you."

"So, am I healed?" Ed asked.

"Medically speaking, you're not healed because the cancer could come back," the doctor answered. "But you've already had a miracle because you're supposed to be dead.

"There is a whole body of controversial material that has been written about cases like yours. We actually have a term to describe you. You are experiencing what we call 'Spontaneous Remission.'"

THE ANSWERS COME

Ed knew he had experienced a miracle, but according to his theology, it wasn't supposed to have happened. He needed answers.

Over the next few months, Ed discovered Creflo A. Dollar Jr., a minister from Georgia, on television. One morning while fixing Martha breakfast, Ed heard Creflo say, "You all know that I was healed of prostate cancer." Ed stopped what he was doing and listened to every word. So when Creflo said that Kenneth and Gloria Copeland were his spiritual parents, Ed wanted to find out who the Copelands were and what they had to say.

The next week, Ed tuned into the Copelands' *Believer's Voice of*

Victory broadcast on WGN out of Chicago. That morning Gloria Copeland was teaching on divine healing.

"She started from scratch, right where I needed to start," Ed said. "She explained the Word for me, and I began to understand healing. She told me to meditate on it. She told me to say it. For the first time, I understood what had happened to me, and I believed in healing."

In the forty-five years that Ed had preached the Gospel, he never once preached about healing. He had told everyone about the Cross and salvation. He had pastored five very strong and successful churches, but he had never told his congregations that Jesus wanted them well because Ed hadn't known it himself until Gloria taught him that morning.

"Gloria was really a special messenger for me," Ed said, his voice cracking. "I am so grateful for her. If Gloria hadn't taught me about healing, I still wouldn't know what God had done for me or how to continue walking in my healing."

SPREADING THE WORD

Now, when Ed is invited to speak at various churches, he always shares his testimony, preaching healing with great boldness. At age seventy-one, Ed is not too proud to say his original thinking about miraculous healing was wrong.

"I just didn't know," he admits, "but God knew, and He healed me in His great mercy."

Ed wants others to experience God's healing power, too. He shares his story every chance he gets—with friends, in churches, at ball games, in restaurants—wherever there is an opportunity.

"I tell them the greatest miracle of all is when you're saved, but God wants to heal you spiritually *and* physically."

Chapter Five ~ Love Is Not Proud

"His Word works," Ed said. "I know it does because it worked for me. Cancer is supposed to be incurable, but I'm living proof that it is curable. According to the doctors, I am in spontaneous remission, but according to the Word of God, I am healed!

"It's just like Gloria teaches: All you have to do is receive your healing like you received your salvation—by faith. That's what I've done."

Pride. While that word conjures up images of haughtiness and vanity, pride can also mean being afraid to admit you're wrong. Sometimes that's the easiest kind of pride to fall into because somehow it seems right—even justified. But no kind of pride is okay. The Bible says that pride comes before a fall. In Ed Dorsey's case, that fall could've meant death. If he had allowed pride to close his eyes and heart to miraculous healing, he probably wouldn't have lived to share his testimony. If he had clung to his original theology about healing, he would never have been able to receive his miracle.

Sometimes it's difficult to admit that our thinking has been errant—especially if that thinking is deeply rooted in our very belief system. God wants to remove the pride blinders from your eyes and show you the truth in His Word. Find out for yourself what the Bible says. Don't let someone else tell you what to believe. God is a personal God, and He will reveal himself and His promises to you if you'll only let Him.

If you're walking in pride due to faulty thinking, or if you've fallen into thinking that you're better than someone else, confess it before the Father right now. He wants to free you from your prideful spirit because He has a miracle waiting just for you.

FOR FURTHER STUDY: Read 1 Samuel 2:3; Proverbs 6:16; Jeremiah 13:15; Mark 7:20-22.

CHAPTER SIX

LOVE IS NOT RUDE

*Looking for Opportunities
to Share God's Love*

Chapter Six Love Is Not Rude

As a retired businessman, Walter Medlock is now enjoying those golden years—playing a little golf, watching sports on television, and enjoying his family. He spends a lot of time at home relaxing in his easy chair, so one would think he wouldn't have much of an impact for God. Not now. He's retired. Leave it to the younger men and women to do God's work.

Walter could take that attitude. After all, he and his wife, Marion, taught Sunday school for more than thirty years at the Free Methodist Church in Bedford, Indiana, and he has served in a church leadership role for most of his life. But Walter doesn't think it's time to hang up his hat and spend his remaining years doing only what he wants. He isn't retired. He's refired and still working for Jesus.

When Walter, who is seventy-seven, wakes up every morning, he asks God for opportunities to share His love. He asks God to make him sensitive to His leading so that he will recognize those opportunities when they arise, and God has been faithful to do so.

SEIZE THE MOMENT

One of those opportunities came in June 1999. The air conditioning unit in Walter's house had been acting up, so he had called a repairman to come and take a look at it. The man arrived at the house early in the morning while Walter was having his devotions. Just as soon as the man stepped into the house, Walter felt that familiar tug on his heart.

It was the Holy Spirit.

"I knew that the Lord wanted me to say something to this gentleman, but I didn't know what, so I just prayed the whole time he was in the other room working on our unit," Walter said.

After about forty-five minutes, the man presented Walter with a ticket that listed all the work he had completed. It needed Walter's signature. As he reached for the man's pen, Walter seized the moment.

"You know, from the minute you walked into our home, the Lord has been impressing on me to talk to you," Walter shared. "I wonder if it would be okay if I shared with you what I read in my devotions this morning?"

"Sure," the man said. "I've got a few minutes."

So Walter spoke to the man about God's forgiveness—the topic of the morning devotional he had read earlier. As Walter spoke of God's love and willingness to forgive, the man's eyes suddenly filled with tears.

"I've been mad and hurt a long time," the repairman said. Then he began to share his story with Walter.

"I'm a Vietnam Vet. And one night when I was supposed to be on duty, I was given the night off. My buddy filled in for me." Right then his voiced filled with emotion, and he hesitated for a moment. "During that watch, my . . . my friend was killed. It should've been me," he told Walter.

Then he went on to tell of how his friend's family had never forgiven him, and he had never forgiven himself. He had lived with that hurt and guilt gnawing at his soul for many years—it had nearly destroyed him.

Walter leaned close to the man and said, "You can wipe that

Chapter Six ~ Love Is Not Rude

slate clean this very day. Jesus will give you a fresh start, and He will even restore that broken relationship with your friend's family. All you have to do is ask Jesus to be your Lord. Would you like to do that today?"

The man nodded, wiping his tears.

Walter led the man in a simple prayer, and he gave his life to Jesus that day. He left Walter's house with much more than a signed invoice. He left with a new heart and a new freedom that God's forgiveness had worked in him.

ANSWER THE CALL

Another opportunity to share God's love came on a Friday morning in December 2000. It was about midmorning, and Walter was just finishing his second cup of coffee and reading the Bible when the telephone rang.

"Hello, is Mr. Medlock at home?"

Walter instantly recognized the familiar "pitch" of a telemarketer.

"Yes," Walter answered. "This is he."

"Well, Mr. Medlock, you've qualified for a no-annual fee credit card, and you . . ."

Walter patiently listened to her rehearsed speech without interrupting. Then when she was all through, he politely responded, "No, I'm not really interested, but you know what? I was just sitting here reading the Bible when you called, and the Lord just spoke to my heart to share something with you. Would you listen to me for a moment?"

The woman agreed, so he began reading a couple of passages of Scripture to her. As he read, the woman remained very quiet.

After he had shared a few verses, he said, "Honey, the Lord loves you today. Did you know that? He wants to give you a hope and future. That's what Jeremiah 29:11 tells us. He has a special plan for your life."

She began to cry.

"You know, the Bible tells us that all have sinned and come short of the glory of God, but Jesus said if you'll confess your sin, He will forgive your sin and take away all your unrighteousness," Walter gently explained. "Once you accept Jesus into your heart, He takes care of the rest of it."

"But I have done some awful things in my life," she shared. "I don't think that God could save me. I . . . I can't be saved," she said, sobbing.

"We've all fallen short—even great people like Billy Graham," Walter said. "But Jesus wants to take away your sin and give you a new life. Would you like that?"

"Yes," she said, still sobbing.

Walter took another minute and prayed with her. She repeated the simple prayer after him and accepted Jesus into her heart as Lord and Savior.

"God had this whole thing planned," Walter told her, "because the minute I picked up the phone, the Lord impressed on me to speak to you. That's how much He loves you."

Walter wished the woman a Merry Christmas, hung up the telephone, and went back to reading the Bible—waiting for the next opportunity to be used.

"The Lord will use His people to accomplish His work,"

Chapter Six ~ Love Is Not Rude

Walter said. "You don't have to be anything special. You just have to be available."

It's all about perspective. When telemarketers call, especially at inconvenient times, most people are automatically aggravated and respond in a rude manner. It seems almost acceptable to cut them off in midsentence with an abrupt, "I'm not interested," and hang up. But Walter saw the phone call as an opportunity to share about God. If you look for opportunities to share God's love, He will open many doors for you to be used. Start each day like Walter, asking God to give you an opportunity to share His love with someone. It may be a repairman, a telemarketer, your neighbor, or a stranger at the supermarket—God will send them your way if you're available.

FOR FURTHER STUDY: Read 1 Peter 3:8; Mark 16:15; John 1:9.

CHAPTER SEVEN

LOVE IS NOT SELF-SEEKING

Living for Eternal Purposes

> **"AMBASSADOR OF LOVE"**
>
> Ivan Hunter
>
> Born January 12, 1930
> Born again June 3, 1951
> Went home June 4, 1998

HE'S AN AMBASSADOR OF LOVE—

a worker for the Lord.
He has a burden for the lost,
too strong to be ignored.
He's a mighty prayer warrior.
His prayers availeth much.
Each time he prays on your behalf,
you're sure to get a touch.
Whenever anyone needs help,
he's there to volunteer.
Serving God with all his heart
is his full-time career.

Chapter Seven — Love Is Not Self-Seeking

His precious smile and special warmth
put everyone at ease.
That blessed joy he has inside,
he found down on his knees.
He loves to fellowship with God
and with God's people, too.
Each time the people congregate,
you'll find him in a pew.
He has a love affair with God.
He just can't get enough.
Because he knows that God is good,
though sometimes life is tough.
His life's been full of challenges.
He's had more than his share.
But he did not face them alone,
the Lord was always there.
That's why you'll hear him praising God
each time you pass his way.
He's God's ambassador of love—
on call both night and day.

BY MICHELLE MEDLOCK ADAMS
[April 1997]

Chapter Seven ~ Love Is Not Self-Seeking

"Glory to God," Ivan Hunter said, walking toward his truck as the sun was inching up over the southern Indiana hills. "Another beautiful autumn morning...thank you, Lord."

"Hey, Ivan!" a coworker called. "Do you want to go fishing with us? There's a couple of us going after we grab a bite to eat."

"You guys go ahead," Ivan said, smiling. "I've got to call on a special friend this morning who's in the hospital."

"Didn't you do that yesterday?" the man called.

"Yeah, I believe I did," Ivan answered. "You boys catch your limit today."

The man waved to Ivan as he drove away. While his coworkers were off to catch fish, Ivan was on a different kind of fishing expedition. This one didn't involve any worms or hooks or boats. It simply required a willing spirit and the Lord's leading. Ivan had been one of God's best fishers of men for some time. It was the only kind of fishing Ivan had time for, and the only kind of fishing that brought him real joy. Ever since he'd made Jesus his Savior on June 3, 1951, Ivan's life had not been his own.

Harold Charles, youth director at the Bedford (Indiana) Free Methodist Church at the time when Ivan got saved, described Ivan's walk with God by telling a favorite story of his.

"Once there was a beggar standing by the roadside, and he had a bowl of wheat. He saw a rich man in a carriage coming his way. Suddenly, the rich man stopped, and the beggar thought, 'I am really going to get something now.' Instead, the rich man asked,

'Would you give me some of your grains of wheat?' And the beggar thought, 'Why does he want my wheat with all of his wealth?' So he only gave the rich man three little grains. As the rich man went on his way, the beggar looked down where the three grains of wheat had been and saw three pieces of gold. The beggar chased after the carriage, saying, 'Here, take my whole bowl!' But it was too late.

"You know, a rich man named Jesus Christ comes along to every one of us and asks for our bowl of wheat—our lives. Let me tell you something. When Jesus Christ came along to Ivan Hunter, Ivan said, 'Lord, take the whole bowl, my whole life. I'm yours, Lord.'"

And Ivan had that "whole bowl" mentality every day of his life—even during the hard times.

HARDSHIPS AND MIRACLES

Ivan belonged to God from the very beginning because his parents gave him to the Lord when he was only an infant. They had always believed God for everything—especially when crises occurred. Now they would have to believe God to heal their infant son. Ivan became very ill as a baby and had to spend five weeks in Riley Children's Hospital in Indianapolis. But on the day he was scheduled for a life-threatening surgery, God supernaturally healed him.

God had plans for Ivan's life.

When Ivan was only four, he suffered another tragedy—his father died at only thirty-two years of age. Ivan was forced to grow up without an earthly father, but his heavenly Father kept a close watch over him during those developmental years.

Ivan and his mother weren't able to attend church very often during that time because she didn't drive, but after Ivan got his

Chapter Seven — Love Is Not Self-Seeking

driver's license, he took his mother to church every time the doors were open. And even though he wasn't too interested in the things of God, the Lord was certainly interested in him. It was only a few years later that Ivan realized he had a void in his life that only Jesus could fill. That's when he gave God his entire "wheat bowl" and began a new life—completely committed to Jesus.

Just as soon as Ivan gave his heart to Jesus, he wanted to work for the Lord, so he began calling on shut-ins in the community and visiting prisoners in the local jail. He and his calling partner, Barbara, who was also a member of the Bedford Free Methodist Youth Group, were dedicated to doing the Lord's work at any cost. Soon their calling ministry became a real team effort as the two began dating and eventually became man and wife on April 5, 1952.

Together, Barbara and Ivan were a one-two punch against the devil, leading people to the Lord every chance they got. But the devil wasn't going to give up so easily.

"We had a lot of hardships come against us," Barbara remembered, "but Ivan always said that our sufferings just made us a better comforter for others experiencing pain and loss."

One such hardship came when their four-year-old son, Gary, was run over by a truck. The accident crushed Gary's internal organs, and he had to undergo a surgery to reroute his pancreas—a surgery that had never been done before.

"We just gave him to the Lord," Barbara said, remembering. "It was a miracle that he lived, but God had it all under control."

Before long, Gary was back to normal, following in Ivan's footsteps, literally. As Ivan would get up at daybreak and head for the barn to tend to his farm, young Gary would follow right behind him, placing his little feet in the larger footprints of his father. He was following Ivan the same way that Ivan was following his heavenly Father—one step at a time with much enthusiasm.

Just as life was getting back to normal, Ivan suffered yet another tragedy. He lost part of his left hand in a farming accident when his glove was pulled into a corn grinder. Still, Ivan never let it steal his joy. No, he just kept working for God and leading his family in the way of the Lord.

Barbara and Ivan had produced quite a little family. In addition to Gary, they had Sharon, Carol, Doyle, and Joni. It seemed that life was complete. Then in 1968 Barbara gave birth to another little boy, Carl, but he came eight weeks too early and died after only living for three days.

"It was hard," Barbara said, "but God was faithful to bring us through the good times and the bad. Our faith in God kept us going."

The children grew up knowing that God was the head of their household, witnessing many miracles along the way. And any time there was an opportunity to fellowship at church, the Hunters were there. They didn't miss church for anything because Ivan felt that strongly about living a consistent Christian life—not just one of convenience.

Once when Ivan was laid off for two years and money was tight, he stared at his gas gauge, realizing he had just enough fuel in the tank to get to church that night, but not enough to make it back home. Still, he felt that God wanted them in church, so the Hunter family made the long trek into town—by faith. When they got there, the first handshake that welcomed Ivan had a $20 bill in it. God was looking out for his fine fisherman.

"Ivan was a husband and father, held a full-time position in secular employment, and farmed the farm on which they lived.

Chapter Seven ~ Love Is Not Self-Seeking

Few persons had the many responsibilities that Ivan shouldered, yet he never found reasons to excuse himself from church and church positions," remembered Wayne Neeley, a former associate pastor of the Bedford Free Methodist Church. "Somehow Ivan always managed to be there: Sunday morning, Sunday night, Wednesday night, and committee meetings. And he wasn't just a church meeting Christian. His Christian service and witness went with him wherever he was: on the job, in the marketplace, into nursing homes, in jail visitation, and to the elderly.

"And what's more, I never saw Ivan when he didn't have a ready smile and an enthusiastic hello for me. He was always praising his God and loving his Lord. He was a beautiful person. I am just one among hundreds that he has touched."

A former inmate of the Pendleton Indiana Reformatory is another. Ivan put many miles on his car, driving to and from that maximum-security prison to minister to a young man who desperately needed to put his faith in Jesus.

At the request of some godly parents, this young man got a visit from Ivan and Barbara. It was the beginning of a beautiful relationship.

"I have a loving mother and father who visited me every two weeks, and they told me about Ivan and Barbara," the former prisoner testified. "They told me, 'Now this guy is a go-getter. He will try to save you.' I wasn't into that saving stuff. I didn't want to hear it because I was dealing with the big boys, getting beat up and stuff in prison, but I agreed to let Ivan and Barbara come and see me."

During that first visit, Ivan listened to the young man's story and then ever so gently asked, "Son, are you saved? Do you know my Jesus?"

"Sort of," he answered, looking down. "I don't know if I am saved or not."

"I know how we can make sure," Ivan said, grinning.

And then he proceeded to lead that young man to the Lord. Today, that former prisoner is the senior pastor of a small Free Methodist Church in southern Indiana.

"Ivan's and Barbara's cards, letters, and visits kept me going while I was in prison," the man shared. "When I finally got out in 1997, their house was the first stop I made."

MAKING THE MOST OF EACH MOMENT

Ivan loved people, and he didn't want to see anyone miss out on heaven. So he took advantage of every opportunity to tell folks about his Jesus.

"One Sunday we'd go to the jails and have service," Barbara said. "The next Sunday we'd go to the shut-ins' homes and sing and pray with them. Then other times we'd go to the nursing homes and minister... just wherever the Lord led us."

And that's how Ivan lived his whole life—following the Lord's leading.

Ivan served many years at the Bedford Free Methodist Church in various capacities and was eventually appointed the minister of visitation—a title he'd more than earned over the years. Then God called Ivan to pastor the Lyons (Indiana) Free Methodist Church, which was quite a hike from his farm. He drove more than 9,000 miles a year to pastor that church, and he did it for ten years.

No matter what his schedule, Ivan was always on call for those who needed comforting and prayer. He was quite the regular at area hospitals.

Chapter Seven ~ Love Is Not Self-Seeking

"He sat with me at the bedside of my husband the last hours of his life," one woman said.

"For six weeks he came to see my mother and served her breakfast and prayed with her, only missing one day when he was in the hospital himself," another woman chimed in.

That was Ivan.

And even when he was diagnosed with cancer and had to be admitted into the hospital on several occasions, he was still on duty. The nurses couldn't keep him in his own room. No, he'd wander the halls and pop his head into other rooms to see who needed prayer. That was Ivan's heartbeat.

"You couldn't talk to Ivan without hearing about God's goodness. He'd always say, 'Taste and see that the Lord is good,'" said Marion Medlock, who knew Ivan for more than thirty-five years. "His face always shone as though he had just been with Jesus. He had that light about him.

"Truly, Ivan gave more than anyone I've ever known, and he never took credit for any of his good deeds. Everything he did, he did for the Lord."

Ivan spent his entire life doing God's will, never giving a moment's thought to his own desires, and he worked for his Lord until God called him home in 1998.

"When I think about Ivan," said Darold Hill, a pastor in the Free Methodist Conference, "I think about the old family motto that used to hang in our log cabin in the upper peninsula of Michigan where I grew up. It read, 'Only one life twill soon be past. Only what's done for Christ will last.' As the years roll by, I am more convinced of that motto than ever before. Life passes quickly, and Ivan is a reminder to all of us to live our lives for eternal purposes."

Living the LOVE Chapter

I have special memories of Ivan, too. Growing up in the Free Methodist Church in Bedford, Indiana, I was privileged to be a part of his kids' church services on Sunday mornings. He'd bound into service, wearing his "Jesus Saves" pin, and lead singing with more energy than any of the first to sixth graders in the room. He'd belt out, "I love Jesus better than ice cream, and ice cream is mighty good," as we giggled at his silly song.

It's been more than twenty years since I was in those services, and though I don't remember much of what he said, I will always remember that he loved me. As a ten-year-old kid, that spoke more to me than any sermon ever could.

His constant joy and genuine love for people made folks say, "Ivan, there's something different about you. How come you're so happy all the time?" And that would open the door for Ivan to share of his first love—Jesus Christ.

It's hard telling how many people will be in heaven because of Ivan Hunter—probably thousands. He worked tirelessly for the Lord to the very, very end. He is a true example of love in action. You see, Ivan never gave any thought to his own wants, hopes, or desires because his life was all about Jesus.

Maybe you've been a person who has always lived your life for yourself, never giving a thought about others or the Lord. If so, you can do something about it today. Ask Jesus to come into your heart. Ask Him to change your wants and desires to line up with the plans that He has for your life. It doesn't matter if you're ten or ninety-two—it's never too late for God. He wants to fill you with that same joy and love that Ivan had—all you have to do is ask. Do it today, and before long, you'll be singing, "I love Jesus better than ice cream," too.

Chapter Seven ~ Love Is Not Self-Seeking

FOR FURTHER STUDY: Read Psalm 16:11; Ephesians 2:8-9; 3:20; Colossians 1:4; 1 John 4:10-11.

CHAPTER EIGHT

LOVE IS NOT EASILY ANGERED

Being Set Free

From Hurts

Chapter Eight — Love Is Not Easily Angered

Porcelain and wooden eagles adorn Jane's southern Indiana home. In the living room hangs a painting of an eagle with the words "They shall mount up with wings like eagles" written below the majestic bird.

Her husband, John, always liked eagles. He even had an eagle tattooed on his arm from the time when he had served in the marines. After he became a Christian, he wanted to have that verse added beneath it.

"He just never had a chance to get it done," Jane said. "He was kind of embarrassed that he had a tattoo. He thought maybe people would take him the wrong way. I think he regretted getting it done."

John regretted a lot of things from his younger, wilder days.

Before he met Jane (not their real names), he lived life on the edge. But in 1985 all of that changed. He and Jane began dating and soon fell in love. They got married, pledging to love each other "until death do us part."

Life was good, and Jane dreamed of all the special moments she and John would create together to treasure for a lifetime.

Shortly after the wedding day, Jane became pregnant. Nine months later, they welcomed a baby girl to the family. Now Jane's five-year-old son from a previous marriage had a little sister. They were a family and had a whole future to look forward to.

"I'd never been happier in my whole life," Jane reflected.

THE NIGHTMARE BEGAN

John and Jane decided to build a new home that year. John was a skilled builder, so he took on the project by himself, but a couple of months into it, he became ill.

John went to a local doctor and was diagnosed with pneumonia. The doctor gave him some medication and sent him home to rest. After ten days on the strong antibiotic, John's condition hadn't improved at all, so he went back to the doctor. His physician told him that he had contracted the flu on top of pneumonia and prescribed some additional medication. Still, John's condition only continued to worsen.

A week later he was admitted into a local hospital, where doctors ran test after test, trying to figure out why he wasn't responding to the strong antibiotics. One doctor suspected that John had abdominal cancer.

John wanted a second opinion, so more tests were run—including an AIDS test. To his horror, the test result came back positive. He was stunned. He had AIDS! The nightmare had begun. Immediately, John was transferred to an Indianapolis hospital for further testing. As he lay there waiting for the results, wave after wave of anxiety and guilt washed over him. But the tests all revealed the same result—John had full-blown AIDS. Just when he thought life was going well, everything seemed to come crumbling down before him.

After some serious soul-searching, he concluded that he'd contracted the disease from a previous heterosexual relationship before he had become a Christian.

"I couldn't believe it," Jane said. "I just kept thinking, *This can't be happening! Not to us!*"

John's doctors told Jane that she needed to be tested, too.

"I was scared," she admitted. "I didn't want to know."

But she knew she had to find out for her children's sake. She

Chapter Eight ~ Love Is Not Easily Angered

knew if she had the disease, it was likely that her daughter would be infected, too.

Jane went to the South Central Community Mental Health Center Inc., in Bloomington, Indiana, to have her AIDS test. People at that facility explained to her the anonymous testing procedure. They issued her an identification number so her name would never be used. No one would have to know.

She knew it would take some time for the results to come back, but the waiting only increased the battles she was having inside. Worry, anxiety, and anger flooded her soul as she thought about what was happening. And yet as difficult as the waiting was, Jane took every one of her concerns to prayer, seeking the strength she needed from the Lord each day. She needed to be strong for her husband—for her children. She couldn't allow herself to be angry at John, not now, not when he needed her the most. She made a conscious decision that day—*I won't dwell in the land of "what if" and "should've been," because it will destroy us.* She decided to live day to day, clinging to the promises of God that her grandfather had taught her at an early age. Only God could heal her hurting heart, so she gave the hurt, confusion, and fear to Him. She asked Him to walk beside her down the difficult road ahead.

By the end of the second week, she could hardly stand waiting anymore.

"Those were the longest two weeks of my life," Jane said.

She called the mental health center and asked if the test results for her identification number were in.

They were.

The woman told her to come up to the center for their findings, so Jane's father and sister accompanied her to Bloomington.

"My dad had to practically carry me up there," she said.

When they reached the office, they were led into a private room and asked to sit down. The man with the results looked at Jane and said very solemnly, "Your test shows you're HIV positive."

Jane felt as if someone had kicked her in the stomach.

"I couldn't even breathe," she remembered.

The man gently took her hand and said, "This does not mean you are going to die. Don't give up."

He began talking with her about possible treatments and medications that were proving successful, but Jane couldn't listen. She was too overwhelmed by the devastating news she had just received.

Jane's dad and sister spent the next half hour asking many questions, seeking as much information about the disease as possible. Jane sat very quietly, thinking about her children. Now they would have to be tested.

"I was worried sick about my kids," she shared. "Waiting for my daughter's test to come back was horrible. I wasn't so worried about my son because he was from a previous marriage, but our daughter was ours together."

After only a few days, both of the children's tests were in. They were both negative.

"That was the first bit of good news we'd had in weeks," Jane recalled.

Over the next few weeks, John's health continued to weaken. He had been put on life support, drifting in and out of consciousness. Jane didn't go up to see him as often as she wanted. It was too much for her to handle all at once.

She sent word to him about the children's test results. When John heard the good report, his condition began improving. For

Chapter Eight — Love Is Not Easily Angered

days he had worried about his daughter. He was sure she would test positive.

"She's a miracle if you really think about it, because I gave birth to her," Jane said. "God was looking out for us, or else she would have AIDS. John called her 'his little angel' because she is such a miracle."

TREASURED MOMENTS

After seven weeks on life support, John's body began to fight back. He recovered enough to leave the hospital. When he came home, he began attending church and reading his Bible.

"He turned his life totally over to the Lord," Jane said.

She was already drawing her strength from God each day. She had grown up in church. Because her grandfather was a minister, she knew where to turn when the going got tough.

"I couldn't have made it without the Lord," she said. "And my family and friends have given me a lot of support, too."

Jane and John accepted their fate and praised the Lord in spite of it all. They spent time reading the Word together and praying with each other. Those were special times, but there were difficult times, too.

"You get used to being sick," Jane said, pointing to several bottles of pills prescribed to her. "The hardest time I can think of was when we told the kids that Daddy was dying."

The doctors advised the couple to tell the children. Their little girl wasn't old enough to understand, but their son needed to know. The doctors told them he would need time to emotionally prepare for the inevitable loss that was coming.

Shortly after John came home from the hospital, the couple took their son into the living room, and John said, "Honey, you know how you've been seeing all the news about Ryan White and how sick he got?"

The little boy nodded his head and said, "It ain't fair that he died."

"No, it isn't fair. You're right," John continued. "Well, Daddy is sick, too, just like Ryan White."

The boy buried his head in John's chest and cried for a long time. Then the family pulled together and vowed to enjoy the times they had remaining.

READY TO GO

John died in the fall of 1993—six days before his thirty-fourth birthday and one month after Jane was diagnosed with full-blown AIDS.

"He was ready to go," Jane said, her voice cracking. "He wasn't bitter. Before he died he told me, 'Honey, Satan can do anything he wants, but he can't take away my salvation.'"

He also gave her one last instruction.

"He told me, 'Don't ever, ever, ever give up on the Lord.' I didn't intend to."

The song "I Want Us to Be Together in Heaven" was played at John's funeral.

And today—they are.

Jane died in 1996, leaving her parents to raise her children. AIDS may have taken her life, but it never broke her indomitable spirit. She didn't die angry or bitter or regretful. To the very end, Jane was thankful to her God.

The last thing she said to me when I interviewed her was this: "I'm not afraid to die. I'll just be crossing over. You know, I've been

Chapter Eight ~ Love Is Not Easily Angered

blessed. I know my life doesn't look that good right now, but it will someday—when I get to heaven."

Of all the people I've encountered in life, Jane has made the greatest impact on my love walk. The last time I saw Jane, she was covered in chicken pox for the third time that fall, still talking of God's goodness. I was amazed. I looked at this Christian mother who had lost her husband to a terrible disease—the same disease she was fighting—and I wondered how she could have such a love that seemed to radiate all around her. After all, life had definitely been unfair to her. Most people would say she had the right to be angry, but she wasn't. Despite the terrible consequences she and her husband suffered because of previous wrong choices John had made before he was a Christian, they both learned to trust in God in a deeper way. Together they learned that "though our outer man is decaying, yet our inner man is renewed day by day" (2 Corinthians 4:18, NASB).

I had heard that some of the children at school were making fun of her kids, saying terrible things about their situation, and it made me mad.

"Doesn't that make you angry?" I asked her.

"No," she said. "They don't know what they're saying. Besides, I don't have time to be angry. I want to use the time I have left to love."

And that's what she did.

Maybe you're suffering with an incurable disease and you're angry at the world, society, even God. Or maybe you're angry with a loved one, and you've been harboring that hurt and anger for years. I can't pretend to know exactly how you feel, but I can tell you this: God knows, and He cares.

You can give all that anger to God right now. You don't have to carry it a moment longer. God loves you, and He wants to set you free from your hurt and anger. The reason God told us in His Word "to not let the sun go down on our anger" is because He knew that anger would destroy us. Ask God right now to replace your anger with His love, and like Jane, you can spend the rest of your life living in love.

FOR FURTHER STUDY: Read Psalm 37:8-9; Proverbs 15:1; 19:11; Ephesians 4:26; Colossians 3:8.

CHAPTER NINE

LOVE KEEPS NO RECORD OF WRONGS

*To Forgive
With Grace,
Mercy, and Love*

Chapter Nine — Love Keeps No Record of Wrongs

"Mom," said the twelve-year-old boy, standing over his mother.

"What... what is it?" Peaches asked, sitting straight up in bed.

"I'm having another asthma attack," Chance gasped.

"I'll get the breathing treatment," Peaches said, helping her son to the kitchen table. "It'll be okay."

Though Chance's asthma episodes were always alarming, they weren't out of the ordinary. He had suffered with asthma since he was a baby, so this September night in 1996 didn't seem too unusual.

As Chance inhaled the medicine, his eight-year-old sister, Marissa, wandered into the kitchen. She sat next to her big brother, laying her head on the kitchen table.

When the breathing treatment was over, Chance stumbled into the bathroom.

"Mom," he called. "I still don't feel right."

Peaches didn't think he looked good, either. His cheeks were more flushed than usual. He still wasn't breathing easier after the treatment, and he looked strange.

"Chance, honey, maybe we'd better wait a few minutes and give you another breathing treatment," she suggested.

That had always worked before, so they waited together at the kitchen table, and just as she was beginning to administer another treatment, he fell to the floor face first.

"Chance!" Peaches screamed.

Instinctively, she ran to his side, scooping him into her arms.

He was in cardiac arrest.

Peaches raced to the nearby phone and frantically dialed 911 as Marissa stood over her brother, sobbing.

This can't be happening! Not Chance. Not my son!

The ambulance sped into their driveway within just a few minutes.

Oh, God! Oh, God! Don't let him die, Lord!

The EMTs worked feverishly to revive her firstborn child, her only son, her Chance, but he didn't seem to be responding.

"Let's go," one of the EMTs called.

As they carried Chance to the ambulance, Peaches tried to calm Marissa.

"He's going to be just fine, sweetie," Peaches whispered. "I'll call you soon."

She left Marissa with a neighbor and climbed into the ambulance, where the EMTs continued to work on Chance. The sirens blared as they rushed to the hospital. Peaches kept thinking it was all a bad dream, but she couldn't make herself wake up. She so wanted it to only be a nightmare. Then she could wake up, go into Chance's room, kiss him on the cheek, and everything would be all right. But it wasn't a bad dream. It was really happening.

Just then the ambulance jolted to a stop. The doors flew open, and Chance was whisked away to the ER while Peaches was taken to the chapel—not the waiting room.

Two policemen stayed with her.

"Do you have any family that I could call for you?" the female officer asked.

"No," Peaches said, wiping her tears. "There's no one."

Chapter Nine ⁓ Love Keeps No Record of Wrongs

She hadn't been close with anyone in her family for a very long time. Why would she call them now?

They probably wouldn't come anyway, she thought.

"What about a friend?" the officer continued.

Peaches sighed, trying to think. "Uhh, there's a friend in Plano [Texas] that you could call for me," she mumbled, writing down the number for the officer.

Each minute that passed seemed like a lifetime. Peaches wanted desperately to see her son. She needed to hold him, to love him, to be his mother.

"How is he?" Peaches asked one of the officers. "Can I see him?"

"He's fine," the officer replied.

But Chance wasn't fine. Without anyone there to comfort her, they didn't want to tell her that her son had died. Shortly after, Peaches' friend from Plano, her neighbor, and Marissa arrived at the hospital.

"When can I see my son?" Peaches asked the emergency room doctor when he finally came to see her. "I want to see him now!"

The doctor was quiet for a moment.

Peaches could feel her heart pounding as though it would explode.

"He's okay, isn't he?" she asked, almost afraid of the answer.

"I'm sorry," the doctor said. "We did all that we could."

"So what . . . so you're telling me he's dead!" she screamed. "It was just an asthma attack. How could he be dead?"

Chance's regular doctor couldn't believe it either.

"We're not God," he said, crying. "We don't know how or why these things happen. I'm so sorry."

Peaches clung to Marissa, stroking her hair. "It's going to be okay, babe," she said. "It's going to be all right."

But Peaches didn't really believe that. Nothing would ever be all right again. She'd lost her Chance, and she couldn't get him back.

ALL MY FAULT

When Peaches and Marissa finally arrived home, a kind policewoman stayed with them until Peaches' aunt and brother could get there. As the police officers finished their report and her aunt phoned the rest of the family, Peaches held Marissa, staring out the window. The night sky seemed darker than usual—a somber reflection of the circumstances.

It's all my fault, Peaches concluded. *I've committed so many sins in my life, and this is my punishment. I caused Chance's death.*

She thought back over her life—the drugs, the alcohol, the sexual affairs, the stripping, the failed marriages—all of it.

I've totally messed up.

At age twelve Peaches began hanging out with the wrong crowd and had basically been on her own since the age of fourteen, when she moved in with her eighteen-year-old boyfriend. At that point, she dropped out of high school and began working odd jobs to pay for her drug habit. Her life had been in a downward spiral ever since. At age nineteen, Peaches was stripping at a topless bar when she met a handsome biker. It wasn't long before she became his "old lady," and the two of them set up house. Their relationship wasn't a good one. In fact, it was a very abusive one, but it had produced two wonderful gifts—Chance and Marissa—before it ended.

God hadn't been a part of Peaches' life since she was a young girl singing, "This Little Light of Mine, I'm Gonna Let It Shine," in Sunday school. She knew about God, but she certainly didn't know

Chapter Nine ⁓ Love Keeps No Record of Wrongs

His love. Her twisted view of religion had led her to the conclusion that God had taken Chance to punish her for all her wrongdoings.

"I truly felt that everything I had done wrong had caused his death," she said, reflecting. "That night I had to choose which way I was going to go: whether I was going to go the way of Satan and be bitter and mad at God or turn to God to take care of everything.

"I was in the middle of a spiritual battle. On one hand, I had the devil whispering in my ear, 'That's your God for you.' And on the other hand, I had God saying, 'I didn't cause this, but I have your son now. He's safe and happy in heaven with Me.' I was so confused."

A few days after Chance's death, Peaches was left alone to face the future. Her biker friends and drug-using buddies had gone, and the few family members who had been there had also returned home. It was just her, Marissa, and the silence.

"I didn't know if I could survive," Peaches remembered. "I was numb with grief."

She reached for a marijuana cigarette to take the edge off. Peaches had slowly given up using the strong drugs of her past, but she was still using marijuana to get her through life's crises. Marijuana was her only escape from the harsh reality, but even it couldn't ease her loss. The pain of losing Chance was too great.

"I just kept thinking, 'How can one person suffer so much pain in such a short time and survive?'" Peaches remembered. "Within a year, I had lost my mother to an abdominal aneurysm and my son to an asthma attack. It was more than I knew how to handle."

A CHRISTMAS TO REMEMBER

The next few months were extremely difficult. Peaches dropped out of the community college she had been attending and retreated to the confines of her home. She just couldn't get it together emotionally.

"I was very bitter and angry at everyone at the time," Peaches said. "But I was never mad at God. I figured I had made those choices, and now I would have to live with the consequences. I think when you get that honest with yourself, you just open the door for God to do all kinds of things in your life."

Peaches had nowhere to turn but to God. Her friends couldn't offer her any answers—only drugs. Her family didn't seem to care. It seemed all the doors had been shut—all doors except one.

On Christmas Day 1996, Marissa opened the few presents that Peaches had been able to give her, and they sat down together to watch the movie *Toy Story*. Just then, the telephone rang.

It was Peaches' father. She and her dad hadn't been on good terms for many years, but she figured he was calling to check on her. After all, it was her first Christmas without Chance. But that's not why he called.

"He called just to cuss me out," Peaches said. "It was unbelievable the things he said to me."

No sooner had she hung up with her father than the telephone rang again.

This time it was her ex—Marissa's dad.

Surely he's calling to console us on our first Christmas without Chance, Peaches thought, but she was wrong again.

"He called to fight with me, and then he cussed me out, too," Peaches said. "They both argued with me on Christmas Day, at a time when they should have been there to support me or at least leave me alone. They were direct hits—one right after the other. I was devastated.

Chapter Nine ⌒ Love Keeps No Record of Wrongs

"I never contemplated suicide, but if it hadn't been for Marissa, I'm sure taking my own life would've been an option."

Peaches hung up the phone and threw herself onto her bed, sobbing into her pillow so that Marissa wouldn't hear her. Desperate, she cried out to God, "If you are there, you have got to take this pain from my heart! You've got to take this anger from my spirit. You have to take it, God. You've got to help me hold it together for Marissa. I am all she has!"

At that very moment, Peaches realized that she was choosing between insanity and life. Suddenly, everything seemed strangely peaceful. Then Peaches heard that still small voice say, "Stand up and turn around."

She pushed herself up off the bed and turned around. When she did, she saw her reflection in the mirror. She wiped her tears and stared at herself a moment. Then she heard that same voice say, "You'll never be the same again."

Instantly, Peaches felt all the pain and guilt leave her. It was as if someone had opened the floodgate of her heart and released all the hurt, bitterness, anger, and guilt. In their place, God poured in His peace, joy, hope, and love.

"I remember the room actually looked brighter at that moment," she said. "I remember staring at myself in the mirror and thinking that somehow I looked different. I knew something major had happened to me."

Peaches raised her hands toward heaven and thanked God, promising to spend the rest of her life being grateful for what He had done for her.

Later that afternoon, some of Peaches' old drug buddies invited her and Marissa to join them for Christmas dinner, so they went.

As soon as Peaches walked into her friend's home, someone offered her a joint. Without even thinking, she took a hit off of that marijuana cigarette, and it sent her to the floor.

"I dropped to my knees for the second time that day," Peaches said. "I started throwing up and shaking—all from one hit off a single joint!"

She knew a joint couldn't affect her that way. None of her other friends were having that kind of trip. It was something or Someone else.

Again, she heard that inner voice say, "Choose life, choose now." Peaches didn't know what to do. She wondered if anyone else had heard that voice.

"It was really freaking me out," she said, remembering. "I stood up, and all my dope friends were staring at me. They didn't know what was going on, and to be honest, neither did I. I dismissed myself and Marissa, and we went home."

Later that week Peaches shared her Christmas experience with one of her drug buddies. She had to tell someone.

"There's no doubt that God has done a work in you," her friend said, "but I don't want any part of that life."

"That's okay," Peaches answered. "I'm not asking you to change, but I just wanted you to know that I am not staying away from you guys because I am mad at you. I just can't be around you anymore. I can't use drugs anymore. God has changed me."

That week, Peaches and Marissa found a church to attend.

"I was jumping into the River of Life, and I had Marissa's little hand in mine," Peaches explained. "So much happened to me on Christmas Day that it took almost a year for me to understand all that Jesus had done for me."

Chapter Nine ～ Love Keeps No Record of Wrongs

FINDING FORGIVENESS, GIVING FORGIVENESS

Peaches began reading her Bible and discovering more of God. The Word healed her hurts one at a time, and God taught her many lessons. One of those lessons came during the summer of 1997. She had just finished reading the passage about Jesus hanging on the cross and suffering for mankind's sin, when a verse she had read many times before seemed to leap off the pages: "Father, forgive them, for they know not what they do." Peaches bit her lower lip and closed her eyes. She knew what she had to do: She had to forgive all those in her family who had ever hurt her.

"I didn't want to do it," Peaches admitted. "I had carried those hurts for a long time, but I knew that if I was going to receive true forgiveness for my wrongdoings that I would have to forgive them first.

"I started forgiving my family by faith. The first few times I tried to do it, it was difficult, but God would remind me, 'Remember the cross,' and I would go ahead with it."

One by one, God helped Peaches forgive the family members who had deeply hurt her. Then came the really tough one—she had to forgive the father of her children—the man she had considered her enemy for the past nine years.

He was seeking to restore a relationship with Marissa, but Peaches wasn't exactly enthusiastic about the idea. She wanted to keep Marissa far from him and protect her from all the hurts she had suffered at his hands. But God had other plans.

"It was time," Peaches said. "I had to forgive the father of my children, wipe the slate clean, and see him through the eyes of Jesus. I didn't want to pass on any bitterness or anger to Marissa. This was the next step in the healing process."

Just as Jesus had prayed to the Father, Peaches prayed, "Father, forgive him, for he knows not what he does." At that moment, she knew she had truly forgiven him. They weren't just empty words. They were words of life.

It was the last piece of unforgiveness she had been harboring in her heart, and suddenly it was gone. For the first time in a decade she felt good, really good on the inside.

Peaches had made the first step on that road to forgiveness, and God was there to walk with her the rest of the way. Every time she wanted to get angry with her ex, God was right there, showing her the way of love.

Today, Marissa, age fourteen, has a good relationship with her daddy. They spend quality time together on a regular basis. And Peaches has faith that God is doing a work in his life.

"God took me out of the miry clay and made me into a vessel fit for His use," Peaches said. "And He showed me that He sees my ex the same way. I can sit here today and honestly say that I have no hard feelings toward him. In fact, I pray for him every day."

A LIVING TESTIMONY

Peaches continues walking in forgiveness and experiencing unconditional love from her heavenly Father. She loves to share what God has done in her life and how forgiveness brought healing, hope, love, and peace to her broken heart.

"I tell people that God is no respecter of persons and that He will do the same for them that He did for me."

Today, she shares her testimony at churches, women's correctional facilities, women's meetings, and biker Bible studies. She feels called to minister to those who think that God could never

Chapter Nine ⁓ Love Keeps No Record of Wrongs

forgive them because of their terrible pasts.

"Once I realized that God didn't take Chance to punish me for my sin, it freed me from so much guilt and condemnation," Peaches explained. "I want others to realize that my God is a good God. He doesn't bring tragedy to teach us things. He brings love and restoration, not guilt and condemnation. He has enough forgiveness for all our sin.

"The Lord showed me that He has totally forgiven me and that He has forgotten all that stuff. So if He has forgotten my sin, why shouldn't I?

"I don't know where I'd be if I hadn't met Jesus on December 25, 1996, but I know this: I wouldn't want to live one day without Him. Someday, I'll get to see Chance again in heaven, but until that time, I plan to do my part to bring a whole bunch with me into the kingdom."

The devil is a liar. Did you know that? For years the devil has been deceiving Christians into thinking that God is the bad guy, that God is the one bringing sickness and death on people to teach them things or punish them for their wrongdoings. That's just not true. Why would God send His Son to die on the cross for our sin, sickness, and disease if He was going to send sickness and death back on us? He wouldn't. God is a good God. Don't let the devil convince you otherwise. Peaches was initially fooled into thinking that God had taken Chance from her, but she didn't remain in the dark for long. God delivered her and poured out His unconditional love on her. He wants to do the same for you.

The Bible tells us that love keeps no record of wrongs. In other words, God keeps no record of wrongs. When you ask God to forgive you for your sin, He not only forgives you, He remembers your sin no more. Isn't that good news? It sounds great when you're on the receiving end of forgiveness, doesn't it? But it's not quite as appealing when you have to forgive others with the same grace, mercy, and love.

If you've been harboring unforgiveness in your heart against someone, you can give that to God right now, and He will replace it with love. Forgiving others is really difficult—especially when you feel that you're justified in being hurt. Your friends may tell you that you have the right to hold unforgiveness against your ex-spouse, your mother-in-law, your boss, or your former best friend, but God sees it differently. He tells us to forgive others so that He can forgive us.

You may not feel like forgiving that person right now. Neither did Peaches, but she forgave her family *by faith*. You can do the same. Say the words, and eventually your heart will follow. Forgiveness is a beautiful thing, and better than that, it's a God thing.

FOR FURTHER STUDY: Read Matthew 5:23-24, 44; Luke 6:27; Romans 12:14-21; Ephesians 4:32; Colossians 3:13.

CHAPTER TEN

LOVE DOES NOT DELIGHT IN EVIL BUT REJOICES WITH THE TRUTH

*Never Lose Heart
When Confronting Darkness*

Chapter Ten — Love Does Not Delight in Evil

"All right, listen up!" demanded six-year-old Lauren, looking her three-year-old brother and sister right in the eyes. "Grandma is watching us while Mom and Dad are on vacation. And remember, Grandma puts up with nuthin'!"

Mary Lou Bogert chuckled to herself as she listened to her granddaughter's accurate description.

It's true—Mary Lou doesn't put up with any nonsense, and that's what makes this sixty-five-year-old grandma so good at the job God has called her to do.

REFIRED, NOT RETIRED

Most people look forward to their retirement years so they can kick back, play a little golf, and enjoy long, lazy afternoons sipping iced tea.

But not Mary Lou.

"I wanted to do something more important with my life," she said. "My children were grown and I had the time."

So in 1994 Mary Lou became involved with the Arapahoe and Douglas Counties (Colorado) Sheriff's Department Victim Assistance program for abused women and children. Later, she went through the necessary training to become a child abuse investigator for the sheriff's department, serving in that capacity until 1998.

"I had always been a housewife and a stay-at-home mother," Mary Lou said. "All of a sudden I had a new career. I guess you could say I was a late bloomer."

Meanwhile, the pastoral staff at Mission Hills Baptist Church in Greenwood Village, Colorado, asked her in 1996 to begin Home and Health Ministries—a ministry for those in need of food, supplies, counseling, protection, financial assistance, medical attention, and clothing.

Since then, Home and Health Ministries has become state licensed, gained nonprofit status, and ministered to hundreds of hurting people—teenage mothers; people who can't pay their bills; those who've been kicked out of their homes; battered women; abused children; newly released prisoners; those suffering with disabilities; widows and many more.

Like Mary Lou, other retired professionals have come out of retirement to volunteer for Home and Health Ministries—all under her able direction.

"We currently have two nurses and one doctor on call, a child psychologist, and a signer/interpreter for the hearing impaired," she said. "In all, we have about forty volunteers who work for us."

Even with forty dedicated volunteers, the workload is heavy because Home and Health Ministries assists close to nine hundred clients a year.

"We have our hands full," Mary Lou admitted. "Sometimes it's discouraging, because for every person we do help, ten more are waiting for some kind of assistance. We make a difference one client at a time."

Like the single mother who needed to have brain surgery but had no one to watch her children until Mary Lou stepped in.

"We just received a wonderful thank-you note from her," Mary Lou said, sorting through her notes and cards to find it. "She wrote: 'I don't know where we'd be without your help. I had no one else to turn to. Thank you so much.'"

Chapter Ten ~ Love Does Not Delight in Evil

Home and Health Ministries was able to fix this single mom's car, pay her bills, and even provide supervision for her two children during those days of surgery and recovery. Mary Lou personally watched over the children.

"What can I say?" Mary Lou said, smiling. "I love what I do."

TOUGH LOVE

But the job isn't always fun. Sometimes it's very tough.

Mary Lou spends much of her time working with battered women and abused children, walking them through the court system, conducting investigations when needed, counseling, assisting in treatment planning, and offering lots of love to hearts that have been broken.

"I can be your best friend or your worst enemy," Mary Lou said. "I step on a lot of toes, and people know it. I have that reputation in the church and in the community, but that's okay. I can't help if I can't get at the truth."

So when Mary Lou suspects child abuse, she goes after the truth with everything she's got.

"All of these kids are my kids," she said. "Every single one of them is important to me. They know that I love them."

That's why it's so difficult when Mary Lou has to watch a child returned to an abusive home due to a judge's wrong thinking.

"We can only do so much," Mary Lou admitted. "If the judge sends the child back to the parents, I'm done. I can't do any more through the courts, so I just cover the child in lots of prayer. I give the child a big hug good-bye and whisper, 'I'll be praying for you.'

"I have to give the situation to God and let Him take care of it. In this line of work, you have to learn to trust God. Someday He will have His justice, and knowing that is comforting."

Sometimes that's the only comfort she has in certain situations, but it's enough. Mary Lou has learned that she can't fix every problem she encounters. She can't mend every broken heart. She can't help every person. But God can. And He has proven himself over and over again.

That's why she tries to introduce her Jesus to every client who is willing to listen to her.

"We've had several give their hearts to Jesus over the years," she said. "When I sense an openness with anybody, I give them a little book to read called *Your Heart Is God's Home* and I invite them to church.

"I tell them, 'When you come to church, you tell the usher that you want to sit with Mary Lou, and he will seat you right next to me. They know where I sit.'"

No matter how smelly, how poorly dressed, or how tattoo-covered they are, Mary Lou sits next to them and nurtures them in the Lord.

"It's a big time investment," she explained, "but it's worth it because it is an eternity investment. It's all about God. That's why I am in this kind of work."

Mary Lou's efforts with Home and Health Ministries have not gone unnoticed. In June 1996 she was given a beautiful wooden plaque with the inscription: "Mission Hills Baptist Church Faithful Servant Award. *His Master replied, Well done good and faithful servant, you have been faithful in a few things. Come and share your master's happiness* (Matthew 25:21)."

"I was very pleased and honored to receive that award," Mary Lou admitted, "but I'd be doing this even if no one noticed. It's what I was born to do."

Chapter Ten — Love Does Not Delight in Evil

MORE TO DO

She just wishes she could do more. Mary Lou's heart hurts each time she sees a battered woman return to an abusive relationship, and she sees it happening all the time.

"Abuse is everywhere," she said. "It's not just in the lower-class families. You'll find it in all kinds of families, rich or poor, and the church as well."

Mary Lou works tirelessly to repair each battered woman's self-esteem and provide her with the resources she needs to get out of the bad situation.

"Telling an abused woman that 'God will take care of it all. Hang in there,' is not enough," she said. "That advice won't work if a woman is being beaten every day. We have to do more.

"I would like to see more churches become involved in community affairs. People need to know they can come to the church for help without any fear."

With that same principle in mind, Mary Lou is currently working to raise funds for a Christian safe house.

"All the shelters in Denver are government-owned, and I want to do it differently," she explained. "I want to let these women and children know that God does care about them. I want people to find God and His healing love."

And she will not stop until she sees that safe house completed.

"This is what I'm supposed to do with my life," Mary Lou reflected. "A lot of people reach retirement, and they think, 'Now what?' Well, now we can use our hidden talents for God. Anyone can do what we're doing if they'll just open their eyes and hearts and say, 'Here I am, Lord, use me.'

"I mean, I certainly don't look the part for what God has called me to do. I don't have a badge. I don't carry a gun. I look like a grandma who is a pushover, but God called me anyway, and I'm sure glad He did."

When Mary Lou Bogert answered the call to serve the Lord with her whole heart, she had no idea that He would call her to work with battered women and abused children. She had no idea that she would one day counsel former prisoners and pregnant teenagers. All she knew was this: "God called me, so He will equip me." And that's exactly what He's done.

Doing God's work isn't always a cakewalk—especially when He uses us to uncover the truth in the midst of chaos and upheaval. When Mary Lou has to call the authorities to remove a child from a home, it's traumatic for everyone involved. But once the truth is revealed, God can move, and love wins out. When Mary Lou has to get tough with a client concerning a lack of integrity or poor parental skills, sharing that truth is not easy. But the Bible says, "The truth shall set you free." And freedom paves the way for love and peace.

Sometimes the tasks that God puts before us are uphill battles, but God's love is more than enough to win those battles. So if God has positioned you in a job where you are the truth-seeker in the midst of evil or the only light in a dark situation—don't lose heart. Don't ask, "Why me, God? Can't you find someone else?" Instead, pray for wisdom and strength, and most importantly, pray for more of His supernatural love. Then, like Mary Lou, you'll love what God has called you to do, and you'll affect many lives for the kingdom of God.

FOR FURTHER STUDY: Read Psalm 19:8-14; Proverbs 3:4-6; 12:17; Luke 9:62; 10:2; John 1:4-5.

CHAPTER ELEVEN

LOVE ALWAYS PROTECTS

*Living in
the Shelter
of God's Presence*

Chapter Eleven ~ Love Always Protects

Tim Oliver emptied his jacket pockets over the bed, unloading the ten boxes of cold medicine he'd just stolen from a nearby drugstore. One by one, he opened the packets. There were about one hundred pills in all.

This will be my final escape, the sixteen-year-old thought.

An escape from his parents' divorce, from drug and alcohol addiction, from all the hurt and pain that had gripped his life.

Tim swallowed the pills and waited to die. His heart pounded so hard, he felt as though his chest would explode. Suddenly, the room became a blur, and Tim drifted into a place he'd been so many times before—the land of hallucinations.

"I remember hallucinating a lot, but I didn't die," he said, remembering. "It was like I couldn't even die right."

When Tim awoke, he was angry. He was determined to kill himself one way or another, so he began using every drug he could get his hands on—marijuana, crystal meth, cocaine, heroine—anything to escape reality.

"I hated reality," he said. "Reality was that I was a drug addict; that I was a high-school dropout; that my parents were divorced. I felt betrayed by everybody—my family, my girlfriend, even God."

Tim had known a lot about God. He had gone to church as a little boy. In fact, the whole family had attended church until his father grew tired of religion and walked away from church when Tim was about seven years old. Soon after, the whole family quit attending church, except for Easter and Christmas services.

"I always thought I was a Christian because my grandfather and my uncle were preachers," Tim shared. "My whole family had always been Christian-oriented. I guess I always believed there was a God, but I never really knew Him."

ROAD TO DESTRUCTION

Tim's daily routine had become a vicious cycle: get up, get high, go to sleep, get up again, get money for more drugs, and get high again. Day after day it was the same. And one bad choice after another had led him down the road to destruction. His mother, Dawn, knew he had a serious addiction problem, but it was all she could do just to provide for him and her two daughters. When Tim's father had abandoned them, their income had been cut in half.

The times Tim didn't have money for drugs, he turned to alcohol for a buzz. One night in May 1999, Tim got drunk and decided to take his mother's 1996 Camaro convertible out for a spin. He drove by his girlfriend's house and, reluctantly, she went for a ride with him.

As Tim approached a stoplight in Cedar Park, Texas, he saw a buddy of his in the car next to him. They revved their engines. Then Tim gave the knowing head nod and slammed the accelerator to the floor. His friend did the same. As tires squealed, Tim's girlfriend screamed. Within seconds the speedometer topped 100, then 110.

When Tim glanced down to see how fast he was going, the needle was pushing the 120-mph mark. That's the last thing he saw before he lost control of the car and sped off the road. The air bag released as the car flipped sixteen times. Breaking glass, cracking branches, the smell of pine trees—that's all Tim remembers until waking up sprawled across the hood of the car. His upper torso hung over the side of the crushed Camaro.

Chapter Eleven ⁓ Love Always Protects

Oh no! What have I done?

As Tim slid off the car, intense pain raced through his body. Every movement was a struggle, but he had to find his girlfriend.

Tim crawled only a short distance before he collapsed. Slowly lifting his head, his eyes focused on a small white cross just a few feet from him. It was adorned with pink flowers and had some writing on it: a man's name and a date, "April 1999."

Am I dead? Is she dead? Then he heard a wailing siren off in the distance.

Moments later, the police arrived at the scene of the accident. They began asking Tim questions, but Tim could only say, "Where is my girlfriend? Is she okay?"

Then he saw her—still trapped inside the crumpled car.

"I saw blood coming down her face, and I thought I had hurt this girl that I cared so much about," Tim remembered.

His girlfriend had suffered a deep wound to her face, but she was miraculously still alive. After seeing the twisted heap of metal, paramedics could not believe that anyone had survived the crash. A man had been killed in a car accident at that very spot only weeks before. The cross Tim had seen had been placed there in memory of the man who had died.

Tim had suffered a broken back in the accident and was flown to a hospital in Austin, Texas. His grandmother Nancy Manley rallied her praying friends, and many began calling out Tim's name to God, standing on the promises in the Bible for Tim's total healing.

A WAKE-UP CALL

Tim drifted in and out of consciousness for several days. The pain was intense. The X-rays that were taken showed that his third lumbar had been crushed and would require extensive back surgery.

Tim's mother was a nurse, so she knew the severity of her son's injuries. She also knew that a nineteen-year-old in the same hospital that week had suffered a similar injury and was paralyzed from the waist down. Still, Nancy and many others believed God for Tim's healing.

To the shock of all the medical staff, Tim walked out of the hospital ten days later.

"I knew it was a wake-up call," Tim said. "Even though I was totally messed up, I prayed and thanked God for another chance. I knew it was His protection that had saved my life."

Tim was happy to be home, but he was still in a lot of pain emotionally and physically. He longed to spend time with his girlfriend, but that wasn't going to happen. Not now. Not since he had almost killed her because of his irresponsibility. She could no longer live with his substance abuse problem, and he couldn't promise that he would give up his habit because he wasn't sure it was a promise he could keep. He didn't want to hurt her anymore. So they ended their relationship, even though they still loved each other.

Tim was depressed. And his body craved stronger drugs than the prescription medicine he was taking. Finally, he couldn't take it anymore. Tim called a buddy from his past to get drugs. Before long, Tim was buying up to $300 worth of drugs at a time, staying high most of the day.

In those few hours of reality each day, Tim thought about his life. He couldn't believe what he had become.

"God had done a miracle for me, but I couldn't live for Him," Tim confessed. "I didn't know how to find God. He just seemed too out of reach for me."

Chapter Eleven ~ Love Always Protects

TOTAL RESTORATION

When August rolled around, Tim accompanied his mother to Fort Worth to visit his grandmother and other family members. It just happened to be the same week of the 1999 Kenneth Copeland Ministries Southwest Believers' Convention in downtown Fort Worth. Tim's cousins were already planning to attend the teen meetings at this weeklong Christian convention, so they asked him to join them. Tim wanted no part of it, but he didn't want to stay home alone either, so he reluctantly got dressed and headed downtown for the convention. He wandered into the teen ministry auditorium and slid into a seat in the back row.

Joseph Canfield, one of the youth pastors of Eagle Mountain International Church, gave an opening talk and then introduced the teen drama team. The troupe of young actors that came on stage to share their faith grabbed Tim's attention because he had always possessed a love for acting.

The drama team performed skits that really stirred Tim. He could relate to the message they were trying to convey through drama. So when Pastor Joseph asked if anyone in the auditorium needed prayer, Tim wanted to go down front and say, "Yes, I need prayer. I need God. I need a new life," but his feet wouldn't move. He could feel his heart pounding really hard, but this time it wasn't from drugs. It was the conviction of the Holy Spirit. Tim wanted to get right with the God who had delivered him from death just weeks before.

With tears running down his face, he went forward, fell to his knees, and cried out to God. Several others joined Tim. Pastor Joseph addressed them all, saying, "If there is something you want to lay down, we want to pray with you."

When Pastor Joseph came to him, Tim said, "I want to give up drugs, alcohol, smoking—my whole life."

At that moment, Tim asked the Lord to make something of his life and give him a clean start.

"I felt clean for the first time in several years," Tim said. "I didn't feel guilty anymore."

Later that week, Tim went forward again—this time to pray for healing. He hadn't been able to bend over since the accident, and he had been in constant pain.

"I knew God could do another miracle for me," Tim said.

When the pastoral staff laid hands on Tim, he felt warmth rush through his spine. Immediately, he bent over and straightened up. He did it several more times—all pain free! Tim ran to the back of the auditorium and did handstands and cartwheels, rejoicing over his healing. He left that convention totally restored—spiritually and physically.

ANOTHER BATTLE, ANOTHER MIRACLE

Upon returning home, Tim had a lot of challenges to deal with. He was facing a court hearing because of a previous public intoxication arrest. Plus, he had already missed one court date. He was told he would have to spend three days in jail and pay a $600 fine.

The night before his court hearing, Tim spent time watching Christian television and praying to God. He knew that the judge he'd been assigned had a reputation for being tough, but he trusted God to protect him once again. As Tim entered the courtroom, he didn't feel alone. He knew that God was with him.

"All rise," the bailiff said as the judge entered the courtroom.

Chapter Eleven ⌒ Love Always Protects

"Please approach the bench," the judge sternly instructed Tim. "Why did you miss your previous court date?"

"I missed the date because I went to a Kenneth Copeland Ministries Believers' Convention in Fort Worth," he said.

"So what happened to you there?" she asked. "Did you find God?"

"Yes," he answered. "I can't tell you how happy I am now. I can't even tell you in words what has happened to me."

The judge became very quiet. Finally she said, "That happened to me when I was about your age, and I understand exactly what you mean."

Tim admitted that he had been doing drugs and had made many wrong decisions before making the most important one of his life—asking Jesus to be Lord over his life.

The judge leaned forward in her chair, stared at Tim and his mother, and said, "I think Tim would be better off in Fort Worth, going to the church he's spoken of. Use the money he owes this court to relocate to Fort Worth. I think that's best. That's my judgment."

God had protected Tim once again.

Later that month, Tim and his family moved to Fort Worth to begin his new life. Now, at age nineteen, he is engaged to a lovely young woman. He has a wonderful and lucrative job working as a salesman for a computer education school, and he is attending a technical training institute to further his education. And, of course, he is sharing his testimony every chance he gets.

"I never thought I would amount to anything," Tim said, "but God had a plan for me, and He has a plan for everyone. He continues to protect me and love me and make a way for me."

No matter how far you've fallen, God can make a way for you, too. Maybe you are battling drug addiction or alcoholism as Tim did. Or maybe you need healing in your body. Perhaps you have a loved one who has walked away from God and turned down the same road to destruction that Tim was on. It doesn't matter what your situation is, God is there for you. He loves you, and He cares about your situation. The devil will try to convince you that you don't deserve a second chance, that God doesn't love you and that God won't protect you. All of those are lies. We find the truth in God's Word.

The Bible tells us that "love always protects." God is love, and He wants to protect you and your loved ones. As a child of God, you have the right to God's protection. Just call upon His name and run into the safety of His shelter. He's waiting there for you.

FOR FURTHER STUDY: Read Psalms 27:1-3; 103; 116:6; Proverbs 2:8; Daniel chapter 3.

CHAPTER TWELVE

LOVE ALWAYS TRUSTS

*Experiencing Peace
in the Midst
of Adversity*

*"Darling, take care of yourself.
May God bless you all and grant we soon have peace
so we can all come home to things we love and dream of."*
—Excerpt of a letter by Joe Ingle, March 1945

Chapter Twelve — Love Always Trusts

News bulletins of World War II flooded the airwaves. Like the rest of America, Joe and Eloise Ingle of Tunnelton, Indiana, listened to the daily reports. One by one, young men were being drafted from their small southern Indiana town. It really bothered Joe that so many of his friends had enlisted and he hadn't.

One day when Joe came in from working in the fields, he told Eloise that he'd been doing some serious thinking.

"I want to enlist," he said.

Eloise looked at the thirty-one-year-old man who had been her first love and said, "Honey, I want you to be happy. If that's what you need to do, I'll support you."

And that's exactly what she did.

"I knew I had to trust God," she said, remembering. "I had to let Joe do what he thought was right."

Her husband of nine years enlisted the very next day and was assigned to the air force. It was the fall of 1943. Thirty days later, the air force sent him to Westover Field, Massachusetts. She joined him there in November, and they stayed together a few more months before it was time for him to leave for the war.

Joe couldn't tell her when they were shipping out, but somehow she knew.

It was 4 A.M. one March morning in 1944. Eloise ran down to the train station to try to see her GI one last time. She raced alongside the train, pounding on every window, calling out his name.

None of the faces looking down at her were Joe's. She couldn't find him. Just as she was about to give up, a soldier told her to wait a moment and he'd get Joe.

"His buddy told him that some lady was outside hollering for him," Eloise said. "Joe knew it was me and came to the window."

He motioned for her to meet him at the front of the car. She climbed the two steps and leaned her head inside the train to give her husband one last kiss.

"I told him I loved him, and then the train pulled away," she said.

Tears streaming down her face, Eloise watched the train slowly pull away from the station and disappear into the night. "Lord, I trust you to bring Joe back to me," she whispered.

The following day, Eloise boarded another train that took her back to Indiana where she could be close to family and friends.

Eloise didn't know where Joe's unit—the Jungle Air Force 68th Squadron—had been deployed, and she knew that Joe couldn't reveal that information. It was classified. But before he had gone, they agreed to write secrets in code. Using play on words and familiar territories in Indiana, Joe was able to communicate his approximate location to Eloise.

"Somehow," Eloise said, "that helped."

The two of them passed secrets back and forth throughout the war, but their letters were filled with much more than secrets. They were also filled with hope, humor, warmth, trust, and an undying love for each other.

Eloise wrote to Joe every night. She would sit near a window, soaking up the moonlight and scribbling down her thoughts. She wrote about amusing things, the weather, the local news—anything she thought might lift his spirits. Then she'd sign it, "All My Love, Eloise."

Chapter Twelve ~ Love Always Trusts

Joe tried to write every day, too, but there wasn't always time. When he got the chance, he would climb out of his foxhole, grab some paper, and express his love for Eloise. Those letters kept the couple close, though distance and war separated them.

"There were several of us wives in Tunnelton waiting for our husbands to return," she said. "We would all run to the post office four times a day to see if there were any letters for us."

And when there was a letter marked U.S. Army Postal Service, Eloise couldn't open it fast enough. She would read every word over and over again until the next letter arrived.

Sometimes, that waiting stretched into weeks.

At one point, Eloise didn't hear from Joe for six weeks. She knew the mail could be lost or just very slow, but she also knew what every soldier's wife feared—something could have happened to her husband.

"Those were very long and difficult days for me," she said, remembering. "I just had to believe that God was in control. I trusted Him to bring my husband home, and I did a lot of praying."

By June 1944, Eloise was fighting her own war—a private war of troubling emotions. She was very concerned about her mother's deteriorating health and was distressed that she hadn't heard from Joe in over six weeks.

While sitting with her mother one afternoon, her mom noticed Eloise's heavy spirit.

"The boys will be home, honey," her mother comforted. "He'll be home. Don't you worry. He's fine."

TRUST GOD

Thousands of miles away, on a small island, a battle raged

around Joe day and night. But as Eloise's mother had said, Joe was okay, just very homesick.

He was scared, but he never wrote to Eloise about the fear he had to face every day. He couldn't tell her how awful the situation was in the South Pacific. He couldn't tell her that his unit had been bombed by the Japanese for twenty-one days straight. He didn't dare tell her that he wasn't sure he'd make it home alive. So he told her in every letter he wrote that he loved her and "to trust God."

"He had a lot of faith in God," she said, glancing at his picture on the wall. Joe passed away in 1988. "He was a strong man of God."

After twenty-seven months overseas, Joe finally made it home. He arrived in Seymour, Indiana, on December 22, 1945. He couldn't wait a minute longer for the bus, so he took a cab all the way to Tunnelton. He wanted to see the woman he'd dreamed about all those months.

When he arrived home, Joe received a hero's welcome. Eloise embraced her soldier and thanked God for bringing him back to her safe. She also continued to pray for the wives in her town whose husbands had made the ultimate sacrifice for their country.

"I've missed you so much," Joe whispered to Eloise.

"I've missed you, too," she said, holding his face in her hands. "I was so scared that I would never . . ."

"Shhhh," Joe interrupted. "It's okay now. I'm home."

The lovers kissed for the first time in more than two years, thankful they were together once again.

After only being home a few days, the couple attended the annual Christmas Eve play at their church. That night, a terrible electrical storm shook the tiny church. Torrents of rain beat down on the roof as the play progressed. Then a great burst of thunder

Chapter Twelve — Love Always Trusts

shook the little church. Joe instantly shot out of his chair and slid under the pew in front of him, covering his head in total fear.

All eyes fell on him.

Eloise reached down and gently helped him back into his seat, stroking his hair to calm him.

"Nobody snickered," she said, "and I never batted an eyelash. We all knew what he'd been through in the war."

Though Joe died more than a decade ago, his memory lives on through his love letters. Eloise has saved every one. The yellowed, tattered messages fill two large boxes. At age eighty-eight, she still treasures those letters, and she's still trusting God that she'll see her Joe again.

"We had a wonderful life together," she said. "We were married fifty-four and a half years, and we dated six years before that. We just trusted the Lord all of our lives—that's how we made it through all of life's ups and downs. I give all the credit to God."

Eloise learned to trust God in the midst of terror and war. She knew of other wives who had received the official letter they all feared—the one informing the family of a soldier's death. And she heard the daily radio reports of casualties and disaster—still, she trusted God to bring her husband home.

The Bible tells us that "love always trusts." It was Eloise's deep love for God that helped her get through those twenty-seven months that Joe was in the South Pacific. And it was that same love that kept them together for fifty-four and a half years of marriage. Eloise not only learned to trust God, but she also learned to trust Joe.

If you're having trouble trusting God today, you're not alone. Trusting God in the midst of chaos is one of the most difficult things you'll ever do. But if you will ask God to replace your fear with love and truly trust Him to answer your prayers, you can experience the same peace that Eloise has known all these years. It's the kind of peace that only comes from God.

There's an old hymn by William Kirkpatrick and Louisa M.R. Stead that says, "Tis so sweet to trust in Jesus. And to take Him at His word. Just to rest upon His promise. And to know, 'Thus saith the Lord.' Jesus, Jesus, how I trust Him. How I've proved Him o'er and o'er. Jesus, Jesus, precious Jesus, O for grace to trust Him more." There's a lot of wisdom packed into that old song. Put your trust in Jesus, and like Eloise, you will experience a lifetime of love.

FOR FURTHER STUDY: Read Psalms 4:5; 62:8; Proverbs 3:5; Isaiah 12:2; Jeremiah 17:7; Hebrews 13:6.

CHAPTER THIRTEEN

LOVE ALWAYS HOPES

*Faith Overcomes
Against All Odds*

Chapter Thirteen ~ Love Always Hopes

As Pastor Lee Pace of The River of Life Church in Phoenix, Arizona, closed the service in prayer, Tina Caldwell gently placed her hands over her stomach, praising God for the miracle growing inside her.

For years Tina had tried to become pregnant. She and her husband, Clay, had used various fertility drugs, but none had worked. After so many heartbreaks, they decided to quit using all those drugs and simply trust God for a baby. Four months later, she was pregnant.

After such a struggle to conceive, the couple rejoiced in the prospect of having a baby. They thanked God for answering their prayers and began to dream of becoming a family. They thought the battle was over, but it was just beginning.

THE BATTLE BEGINS

Only eight weeks into her pregnancy, Tina began bleeding, and the doctor told her she would probably miscarry.

This can't be happening, Tina thought as she and Clay waited in the Phoenix hospital emergency room. *God gave us this baby.*

As the nurse helped Tina onto the examining table, Tina thought about God's promises.

I know God is faithful. I know His Word is true.

The nurse moved the Doppler wand across Tina's abdomen, searching desperately for the baby's heartbeat.

Baboom. Baboom. Baboom.

"You still have a baby," the nurse said, smiling.

It was the first time Tina had ever heard her baby's heartbeat. It was so fast, so beautiful.

With each heartbeat, Tina's hope grew stronger.

GOD HAD A PLAN

Every day she didn't miscarry, Tina's hope and faith increased. Her condition had been labeled "a high-risk pregnancy," but she thought of it as "a high-hopes pregnancy."

Tina didn't dwell on her condition. She had other important concerns to think about. Clay had been offered an Executive Chef position at a thriving ministry in Fort Worth, Texas, and had prayerfully accepted the offer. The timing seemed off, yet they knew it was somehow part of God's master plan. Tina also looked forward to spending time with her sister, Twyla Pyles, who lived near Fort Worth.

Clay began his new job two days after Christmas 1996 while Tina rested at her sister's house. Through the stress of the move, Tina's bleeding had increased. On New Year's Eve, they found themselves back in the emergency room, this time at a Dallas hospital.

As the doctor smoothed gel over Tina's abdomen, gliding the wand up and down, and from side to side, the Caldwells stared intently at the ultrasound monitor. Just then they saw a glimmer of movement. It was their baby!

"It looked like she was jumping for joy," Tina said, reflecting.

Their baby was healthy and developing.

After that, Tina began seeing her doctor weekly. It was then she discovered that Harris Methodist Hospital in Fort Worth had one of the leading neonatal units in the nation.

"We knew God had us right where He wanted us," Tina said.

Finally, the bleeding stopped during the nineteenth week of

Chapter Thirteen — Love Always Hopes

pregnancy, but it was only the calm before the storm.

In her twentieth week of pregnancy, Tina went in for another ultrasound, hoping for a good report, but something was wrong. She knew it.

Tina lay on the cold table, sobbing, while her sister stood nearby praying silently.

A few minutes later, a specialist came in.

"Tina," he said, "your water has broken, but it's much too early for the baby to be born."

Tina felt numb all over. When Clay arrived, the doctor explained the facts and offered two options: take the baby immediately, or wait for Tina to go into natural labor. Either way, he told them that the baby had little chance for survival.

"We believe in miracles," Clay said. "Let's wait and give God a chance to work."

Tina and Clay went home and prayed for a miracle. Three weeks later, Tina's body went into natural labor. They rushed to the hospital and discovered that Tina's cervix had begun dilating.

A specialist in high-risk deliveries was called in to examine her. After studying her ultrasound, he leaned back in his chair but said nothing. A few moments later, the doctor turned off the machine.

"I'm sorry," he said. "I can't offer you any hope that your baby will survive being born this early."

The doctor left the room, but the finality of his words hung in the air.

Tina was admitted to the high-risk prenatal ward, and they gave her medication to stop her labor, hoping to give the baby more time in the womb. Still, her labor continued and infection set in. The stench of sickness in the hospital room was suffocating. Clay opened the window, breathing in the fresh air and exhaling the hopelessness that was trying to overtake him.

Later that week, on Sunday, February 23, Tina's pain intensified. Since she first started having difficulty, many people were praying for them. Family. Friends. Nurses. Doctors. Strangers. They were all praying for God to perform a miracle.

Still, Tina's condition worsened, and her blood pressure dropped dangerously low.

"You're going to have to make a choice," the doctor told Clay. "If we prolong the baby's birth, Tina's life could be in danger. Her body can no longer tolerate the infection and stress."

"If I have to choose, I'll choose my wife," Clay said, stroking Tina's fevered head.

On the way into surgery, Clay looked at a nearby nurse and said excitedly, "We're going to have a baby!"

"I know," the nurse said, but her serious eyes held none of the joyous anticipation a normal birth brought.

Clay held Tina's hand as the doctor delivered their tiny baby—it was a girl!

Tina instinctively shouted, "God, please breathe the breath of life in her!" At that moment, Clay decided the baby's name would be "Zoë," which means "Breath of God."

Clay had been told the baby would be small, but he was not prepared for what he saw. She was purple. Her ears were only half formed. Her legs were drawn up, and her skin was transparent—so thin her veins and organs were visible.

Baby Zoë weighed only 1 pound, 3½ ounces, and was 6 inches long.

She had a 1 percent chance of survival.

Chapter Thirteen ~ Love Always Hopes

AGAINST ALL ODDS

After Tina was stabilized, Clay staggered into the hospital hallway and fell to his knees. Several nurses cried alongside him.

There was little celebration surrounding the birth of baby Zoë. No picture-taking. No laughter. Nothing.

Later that day, Zoë lay under a heat lamp. Her head, the size of a small lemon, was covered with a tiny pink hat. She was so small that Clay's wedding ring fit over her arm. Tubes and monitors surrounded the little life, but so did the glory of God.

Clay copied scriptures and taped them to Zoë's incubator. Philippians 1:6 became their promise:

> *And I am convinced and sure of this very thing, that He Who began a good work in you will continue until the day of Jesus Christ [right up to the time of His return], developing [that good work] and perfecting and bringing it to full completion in you"* (AMP).

Clay and Tina and the medical staff took one day at a time. And by some miracle, little Zoë continued to survive. During Zoë's first three months, she overcame tremendous medical hurdles.

"Her health changed every fifteen minutes," Clay said. "It was a real struggle to not give in to your emotions."

Against all odds, Zoë thrived. The doctors and nurses could offer no medical explanations, but the Caldwells knew the reason—God, the Great Physician, had taken over and was caring for their daughter.

TESTIMONY TO THE WORLD

Weighing 4 pounds, 3 ounces, Zoë was released from the hospital on June 3, 1997. The proud parents had a Winnie the Pooh nursery awaiting their very special baby.

Today, more than four years later, Zoë is happy, healthy, and attracting a lot of attention. One day, after a woman in a shopping mall complimented Tina on her beautiful daughter, Tina said, "She's a miracle of God," and proceeded to tell the woman Zoë's story.

The woman listened intently and said, "My, she's quite a testimony."

And the testimony of God's goodness to Zoë continues. Everywhere she goes, the Lord opens up a door for Zoë's story of hope to be shared.

"Hope was the knot at the end of the rope," Clay said, kissing Zoë's cheek. "Zoë has taught me much about hope and love. She's made me a better person. She saved my life as much as God saved hers."

Like Clay and Tina Caldwell, all people battle hopelessness and grim circumstances at some point in their lives. In fact, you may be going through what seems like a hopeless situation right now, but don't lose hope. Don't give up. The devil wants you to become hopeless, because if he can steal your hope, he can destroy your faith in God.

God cares for you just as much as He does Zoë. He has a miracle waiting just for you, so don't stop believing. No matter how hopeless your situation may seem, tell God that you love Him and determine today to put your hope in Him.

FOR FURTHER STUDY: Read Psalms 31:24; 33:18-22.

CHAPTER FOURTEEN

LOVE ALWAYS PERSEVERES

*Never Give Up
on the Kingdom of God*

Chapter Fourteen ~ Love Always Perseveres

Pete Williams breathed shallow, nervous breaths as he sat in the getaway car, psyching himself up. He gripped the .357 Magnum with both hands and stared at the floorboard.

I can do this, he thought. *I won't hurt anybody. I'll just go in there, get the drugs, and leave. It'll be easy.*

"Let's go," coaxed Pete's partner in crime.

The two men slipped into the drugstore and pointed their weapons at the man and woman behind the counter.

"This is a robbery," Pete yelled. "Give us your drugs!"

Just then, another employee came in the back door. Pete told him to get behind the counter and sit down. Pete ordered the woman to sit down, too.

"I can't," she said. "I have a bad back. I'm in terrible pain."

"I'll help you," Pete said, gently placing the woman into the chair.

For a brief moment, he felt sorry for his victims. As he stood there with his gun pointed at them, he suddenly heard a voice rise up inside of him. *You don't have to do this, Pete. There's a better way.*

Pete didn't have time to listen. He and his buddy had to escape. They grabbed the drugs and the small amount of cash and ran out the front door. One block later, they were back at the car where the third accomplice was waiting in the driver's seat.

They jumped into the car, and Pete dove into the backseat.

Within minutes lights were flashing and sirens were blaring behind them. The police followed closely and shot at them continuously. Pete lay in the backseat, wishing it were all over. He glanced up at the speedometer—they were doing 110 mph down Interstate 55 in Mississippi.

"Oh, God!" the driver shouted.

The car swerved out of control, spinning right into a tree. Shaken, Pete rolled out of the car and ran into the nearby woods. He hid in some bushes while the police combed the area. It wasn't long before they found his buddy. Pete remained totally still. He could hear the search dogs barking. He'd been injured in the wreck, and at some point, he passed out. When he awoke, four and a half hours had passed. Pete peered through the branches of the bush, surveying the area. Their car was gone. It appeared the police had also gone, so Pete carefully started back toward the highway. After only a few steps, he was spotted.

"Stop! You're under arrest!"

Those words altered Pete's life forever.

Injured and scared, Pete sat in the back of the police car and stared out the window. He wondered if this would be the last time he'd see the free world—the world outside of prison.

Pete was charged with armed robbery in Georgia, Mississippi, and Alabama, and sentenced to 105 years in prison. At age twenty-four, Pete was facing two life sentences without parole and headed for an Alabama prison.

Pete knew his future was grim, but in the midst of it all, he was somewhat relieved that he had been caught. At least now all of the criminal behavior, the running, the lying—it would all cease. Unfortunately, his drug addiction wasn't so easy to stop. It stayed with him. It was a part of him, and it had been since he was a young boy.

Pete had grown up in the projects of Birmingham, Alabama, and started dabbling in drugs at age twelve. By the time he was seventeen,

Chapter Fourteen ~ Love Always Perseveres

he was heavily into heroin. At eighteen he went into the navy, and his drug addiction went with him.

"While I was in the military, the drugs were no longer fun and games," Pete said. "I had to have them."

After three years in the service, Pete was dismissed with an honorable discharge, leaving him with no job or money. He needed funds to buy drugs, and he was desperate.

"I couldn't figure out how to get any drugs, and I'd conned every doctor I could con," Pete remembered. "Then it came to me, 'Drugstores have drugs.' I knew some guys who'd been robbing drugstores, so I asked if I could come along."

Four armed robberies later, he ended up behind bars.

Drugs had driven him there, and that same addiction continued to control his life.

LIFE BEHIND BARS

By the time Pete was sent to Parchman Prison in Mississippi, he had been imprisoned about six years. There were ways to get drugs in prison, and Pete had tapped into those sources. He had tried to quit, but he couldn't. He even tried going to chapel a few times, but nothing seemed to work to break his addiction.

Pete grew angry—so angry, he was plotting to kill another inmate in his unit. But before he could carry out his plan, he was relocated to the prison's treatment center for drug and alcohol addiction.

While lying on his bed that first night in the treatment center, Pete noticed a group of inmates forming a circle in the dayroom area.

"I thought they were fixing to have a fight," Pete recalled. "Then they started looking at me. I thought they were coming after me."

Two of the men walked over to Pete, and Pete hopped up and took his fighting stance. He was ready. He had to fight to live, growing up in the projects. And because of his size—6'1" and 275 pounds—he usually had to fight two men instead of one.

The two inmates came closer, and one said, "Hey, we're going to have prayer here, and we wanted you to know that God loves you. He has a plan for your life, and He wants to meet your needs."

Pete cursed at them. "You're all crazy!" he yelled.

For months they would ask Pete to join them, and he would curse at them and mock them. Every time they asked him to join their group, he told them he wanted no part of it. But one inmate wouldn't give up. He continued telling Pete how much Jesus loved him.

"He'd come into my area and talk to me about God, and I wouldn't even talk back," Pete said, remembering.

Then one day Pete was ready to talk.

"Look, man, you've been talking to me about God and this Jesus stuff for months," Pete exploded. "Now I've got some talking to do."

"Okay," the man answered.

"What are you in here for?" Pete asked.

"Rape," the man said.

Pete laughed at him.

"Man, you don't need to be praying for me," Pete said. "You need to be praying for those girls you raped!"

"I have prayed for them," the man explained. "God has forgiven me and so have they."

Pete dropped his head. He was out of ammunition.

"I'm free and you can be free, too," the man continued. "I'll be praying for you."

Chapter Fourteen ~ Love Always Perseveres

Every night Pete watched that man kneeling beside his bunk, praying.

Pete would holler across the hall, "Don't be getting on your knees and praying for me. It ain't doing no good! Quit wasting your breath! God don't want to do anything for me."

Pete had been reared by moral parents, and his mother had taken him to church almost every Sunday morning, but he had never learned that God loved him unconditionally.

"In Sunday school they taught me that if I did anything wrong, God was going to get me," Pete said. "I thought God sat up in heaven with a big club ready to get everyone who acted mean."

Based on the distorted image of God that Pete had developed, he was sure God was mad at him. He thought he'd blown his chance for a good life, so why bother praying? Still, he couldn't refute God's hand upon his life.

God always seemed to put someone in his path when life seemed overwhelming and hopeless.

"I can remember when I was ten years old someone stopped me on the street and told me that Jesus loved me and that He had died for me," Pete reflected. "I couldn't understand why He had done that. I didn't understand why Jesus would leave heaven and come and die for somebody like me."

A NEW LIFE

As the years of prison life dragged on, Pete grew hopeless, thinking about how he had wasted his life. He didn't even have any support from his family. Right after his sentencing, his wife and children had deserted him. He had the worst job in the whole prison—cleaning toilets. And he was still hooked on drugs after all these years. His life seemed to be over.

Late one night in February 1986, Pete was lying on his bed just staring at the ceiling of his cell.

How could I have messed things up this bad?

Pete didn't know exactly the right words to use, but he prayed the best prayer he knew how: "Lord, if you're real, and you can help somebody like me, I'd like for you to forgive me. I know I've ruined my life, but if you can do anything for a guy like me, I'd appreciate it."

Pete fell asleep, wondering if God had even heard him.

The next morning, Pete woke up and knew that something was radically different inside. He could feel the difference. God had changed him. He no longer craved drugs. His raging anger was gone, and a peace had settled over him. Somehow he knew he would never forget this morning. It was the first morning of a new life for Pete Williams. For the first time in years, everything looked brighter. Pete couldn't wait to find the inmate who had been praying for him.

"I found Jesus," Pete said when he saw the man later. "I'm glad you didn't give up on me."

The man gave Pete a big hug, and the two rejoiced together over what God had done.

Pete was excited about finding the Lord, but now he needed to learn more about Him. So Pete wrote to the chaplain and asked for a Bible. As soon as he received his very own Bible, Pete began reading it for hours every day. Then a fellow inmate loaned Pete a book about faith. Pete devoured it. Next, he started watching Christian television programs and reading Christian magazines. He couldn't seem to get enough. His addiction to alcohol and drugs had now been replaced with an incredible desire to learn and know all he could about Jesus.

Chapter Fourteen ⁓ Love Always Perseveres

He studied God's Word six hours every day and prayed from 4:30 P.M. to 7 P.M. every night. In addition, he finished a three-year Bible correspondence course.

One day while studying his Bible, Pete read Jeremiah 29:11, "'For I know the plans I have for you,' declares the LORD, 'plans to prosper you and not to harm you, plans to give you hope and a future.'"

That verse can't be for me, he thought. *I mean, there's no hope in prison. There's no future in here.*

Pete grabbed his *Strong's Concordance,* his *Vines Expository Dictionary* for the New and Old Testaments, and his *Young's Analytical Concordance* and began researching every word that pertained to prison. When he found Psalm 146:7 that says, "He upholds the cause of the oppressed and gives food to the hungry. *The LORD sets prisoners free,*" Pete knew he had something. He had found a scripture to believe in and stand on for his freedom.

Then he read 2 Corinthians 4:18, where the apostle Paul said, "So we fix our eyes not on what is seen, but on what is unseen. For what is seen is *temporary.*" Pete realized that he had a temporary situation that was subject to change, and he got excited. And for the next nine years, every time Pete went before God in prayer, he reminded God of His promises and praised Him for His love.

"I found that God's love was unconditional," Pete said. "God helped me to see myself as He saw me—not as a prisoner but as His son."

Pete kept studying the Word of God and living a Christian life in the midst of fighting, disharmony, and day-to-day prison hardships. On days when he thought he couldn't take it anymore, he'd remember God's love for him, and peace would fill his heart.

FAITH AND PERSEVERANCE BRING FREEDOM

On New Year's Eve 1994, Pete was in his cell watching the Trinity Broadcasting Network (TBN) while the other inmates watched Dick Clark's Rockin' New Year's bash. As Pete listened to the Reverend Creflo A. Dollar, Jr., Pete heard the words, "1995 is the year of favor!" When Pete looked up, Dr. Dollar was pointing his finger directly at the camera.

"It felt like his finger hit me right in the chest," Pete said, remembering. "I knew something big was about to happen in my life."

Soon after Pete went from cleaning toilets to the best job in the prison—working for the chaplain. Then Pete was asked to share his testimony at churches, school convocations, and civil group meetings. Pete began meeting senators, doctors, judges, lawyers, and other important leaders. It truly was the year of favor for Pete.

One day upon returning to his cell, Pete found a letter on his bed. He ripped it open and read the words, "Send $3.50 to pay for your newspaper ad so that you might be considered for parole."

Pete couldn't believe it. He ran to the telephone to call his case manager.

"Could this be right? I'm not even eligible for parole," Pete reasoned with her.

"It's right, but you better send in that money, or you'll be passed over," she said.

It was several weeks before his parole board hearing, and Pete spent that time praying and confessing the promises he had found in the Bible concerning his situation. When the day finally arrived to go before the parole board, Pete was ready. He walked in and sat down before the parole board. He wasn't allowed to say anything

Chapter Fourteen ~ Love Always Perseveres

except his name, his prison number, and his crime.

"Mr. Williams," one board member spoke, "there is no way we are going to let you out of prison. You are unfit for society."

"Okay," Pete said and walked out.

At that time, Pete had already served fifteen and a half years of his sentence. He knew how the system worked. The parole board would reconvene in four months, and he would get another chance. During that time, Pete continued to study his Bible and pray. And four months later, he was called back before the board for his second hearing.

The board members looked through his file again and said, "There's no way we can let you out of prison."

Pete said, "Okay," and left.

Four months later—same scene, same story.

After he walked out of the parole board hearing for the third time, Pete was angry. He prayed, "Lord, I've stood on your Word for everything, and I believe that you are going to get me out of prison. I don't know what to do about this situation, so I am seeking you for wisdom."

Open your Bible to Proverbs 21:1, Pete heard the Lord speak to his spirit.

Pete flipped through the worn pages of his Bible and read, "The king's heart is in the hand of the LORD; he directs it like a watercourse wherever he pleases."

He turned to his concordance once again and looked up the word "king." He found that it meant "one in authority."

Pete prayed, "Lord, I believe that those parole board members' hearts are in your hands and that I will be shown favor."

The Lord showed Pete one specific parole board member whose

heart was hardened toward Pete—the chairwoman. Pete started praying specifically for her.

He prayed one more request—permission to share his heart at the next parole hearing. He wanted the opportunity to say more than just his prison number and past crimes he had committed.

Four months later, Pete was called back, along with fifty other prisoners. One of the inmates came out and said, "The parole chairwoman ain't in there. All the others are there, but she's not."

Pete paced back and forth, praying as he'd never prayed before. Pete wanted to talk to her. He had spent many hours praying that her heart would not be hardened against him.

By lunchtime the parole board had seen everyone but two people—Pete and one other inmate. They were instructed to go to lunch and return at 1 P.M. Pete went back to his building and prayed all during lunch. At 1 P.M., Pete and the other prisoner waited outside the hearing room and watched as all of the parole board members passed by to enter the room. The chairwoman wasn't with them.

The other prisoner went first. Pete sat with his head down, praying, and when he looked up, he saw her walking by. It was Pete's turn, and she had arrived just in time.

She stared at Pete as he walked in.

"Mr. Williams," she said with a half-smile, "we've seen you three times, and we've done all the talking that we're going to do. Now we want to hear from you."

Pete doesn't remember what he said. He just knows what he said was led by the Holy Spirit, because when he finished, he walked out a free man. That was December 14, 1995. He had persevered. He had believed God. And love had won.

Chapter Fourteen — Love Always Perseveres

After spending sixteen and a half years behind bars, Pete was ready to begin a new life in the free world, and God had a great one planned for him.

PREACHER TO PRISONERS

In 1997 the Lord called Pete to preach, so he began "Captives Set Free Ministries" with a staff of six volunteers. It wasn't long before the ministry grew.

In 1998 "Captives Set Free Ministries" ministered in seven states. In November alone, Pete saw six hundred men make Jesus the Lord of their lives. The ministry continues to grow and reach many inmates inside prison walls.

"We're seeing people set free from drug addiction, healed from diabetes, emphysema, TB, depression—God is working miracles!"

Pete also travels around the country ministering with Mike Barber Ministries.

"I take the message of Jesus to the prisoners—the same message that set me free," Pete said. "I tell them that no matter what they've done or who they've hurt, God still loves them and wants a relationship with them.

"No one visited me for eight and a half years while I was in prison, but I survived because God's love sustained me. He wouldn't let me give up."

Love always perseveres. Pete Williams can testify to that verse. He lived it. He knows it's true. And the Bible says that God is no respecter of persons. So what he did for Pete, He will also do for you and your loved ones.

Maybe you feel unlovable. Maybe you feel as though God could never love you because of your past. Well, I'm here to tell you that He does love you. When the Father looks at you, He sees you through the eyes of love. So forget about your past because God has. He doesn't remember your past sin. The Word of God tells us in 2 Corinthians 5:17 that after you made Jesus the Lord of your life, you became a new creature in Christ Jesus. God sees the new creature that you are, not the old sinful one.

If you haven't ever prayed the prayer of salvation, we can take care of that right now. Turn to Appendix A in the back of this book and pray that prayer with all your heart. You can start fresh today. Isn't that good news? Because of what Jesus did on the cross, He can wipe the slate clean, and you get to start a brand-new life. It's like hitting the reset button on a video game—you get to start over with no penalties. Praise the Lord!

Maybe you're saved, but you have loved ones who are not living for the Lord. In fact, they may be far away from God right now, but don't give up. Just as that fellow inmate wouldn't give up on Pete, and just as Pete wouldn't give up on freedom, even though the parole board had stated he would never get out of prison—don't you give up, either. Perseverance gets results!

Luke 11:8 in the Amplified Version says, "I tell you, although he will not get up and supply him anything because he is his friend, yet because of his shameless persistence and insistence he will get up and give him as much as he needs" (emphasis added).

Get busy on your knees! Pray the prayer in Ephesians 1:16-23 for your unsaved friends and family and keep praying for them until they step into the kingdom of God.

Your persevering love may be their only chance for freedom—freedom from sin and death—so stand with them and love them

Chapter Fourteen — Love Always Perseveres

unconditionally just as God loves you. Let God's love shine through you. And above all, don't give up.

FOR FURTHER STUDY: Read Psalms 13:5-6; 36:5-7; Isaiah 61.

CHAPTER FIFTEEN

LOVE NEVER FAILS

*Enduring
the Storms
of Life*

Chapter Fifteen ～ Love Never Fails

Thirteen-year-old Marion listened intently as the missionary told of her work in Africa. Marion had already given her heart to the Lord, but now she wanted to give her whole life to His service.

"My heart did flip-flops as the missionary spoke," Marion remembered. "I felt the call so strongly. I even told my pastor about it."

No one took Marion very seriously, but she hid that desire in her heart, knowing God would use her in the mission field someday.

Time went on, and Marion finished school and began working at a printing office in Louisville, Kentucky. At age twenty, she seemed to have it all—a personal relationship with God, an education, a good-paying job, and a steady boyfriend. Still, she felt as though something was missing in her life.

"I really wanted the right man," Marion explained. "I wanted the husband God had for me because my walk with God was the most important thing in my life. So I asked the Lord, 'When Mr. Right comes along, please show him to me.'"

As it turns out, "Mr. Right" was working in the same building—she just hadn't met him yet. One afternoon Jim Zirkle walked into the office, and Marion sensed the voice of the Holy Spirit in her spirit, saying, "That's him. That's your husband." Marion stared at Jim, following his every move as he wandered through the office. Just before he headed out the door, he turned in her direction and they made eye contact.

"I didn't even know him," she said. "But I was sure I'd heard God."

Only three days later Jim came back by the office and asked Marion for a date. Even though she wanted to say yes, she answered, "No, not right now," explaining that she was seeing someone else. Jim wasn't satisfied with that answer, so Jim met with her beau to discuss the situation. The discussion became quite heated, and Marion saw some qualities in her boyfriend that she didn't like. She ended their relationship that night, clearing the way for Jim to date her.

The following Friday Marion and Jim went on their first date, and she shared about her call to the mission field. She didn't know when, where, or how it would all come together, but she wanted Jim to know what he was getting into before they began courting. That was in July 1964. Three and a half months later they were married, and Marion's life finally seemed complete.

ANSWERING THE CALL

Marion and Jim were enjoying married life and raising a family when God shook their life up a bit. He called them to Rhema Bible Training Center in Tulsa, Oklahoma, in 1977. So they packed up their family and followed the Lord's leading. During the time they spent at Bible school, they grew and continued to mature in their relationship with the Lord and each other.

God was preparing them for His special plan He had for their lives.

In February 1979, Jim had the opportunity to represent Rhema on a ten-day mission's trip to Guatemala. Seeing God move in a mighty way during that trip radically changed his outlook on life. When he returned to Oklahoma, it no longer felt like home. He told Marion, "I want you to come to Guatemala with me. I want

Chapter Fifteen — Love Never Fails

you to experience what I have experienced. I believe God wants us to be missionaries there."

Ever since Jim had returned, Marion could sense a new excitement in him about reaching those who needed Jesus. She promised Jim that she would pray and ask the Lord to show her what He wanted for them. *But what about the children?* she thought. *How will they react? Is this the best move for them? For us?* And in June the two of them returned to Guatemala to see what God was beginning to do. She told the Lord, "God, if this is from you, and we're really supposed to be missionaries here, then you confirm it."

As Marion and Jim retraced some of the places he had ministered in on his trip, they prayed together for God's direction for their future. It wasn't long before they had His answer—they were called to minister to the Guatemalan people.

At age thirty-six, Marion's dream of becoming a missionary was finally being fulfilled. Though it had taken twenty-three years since she had heard the missionary speak about Africa, God had used those years to prepare her for the work He had for them in Guatemala. She thanked the Lord for the godly husband He had given her and the opportunity to grow and mature in Him through their time at Rhema.

The couple put their things in order, moved their three children, ages eight, eleven, and thirteen, to Quetzaltenango, Guatemala, and began Living Water Teaching in October 1979.

OVERCOMING CHALLENGES

When the Zirkles first arrived in the war-scarred, poverty-stricken country of Guatemala, only 3 percent of the people were Christians. Many had never even heard the gospel. Marion and Jim were so excited, so full of zeal, so ready to tell the Guatemalan people all about Jesus, but there was just one problem. The Zirkles only knew eighteen words of Spanish. But that didn't stop the Word from going forth.

The Zirkles went from village to village showing T. L. Osborn films that were translated in Spanish and singing the only hymn they knew in Spanish, "I Have a Friend Who Loves Me. His Name Is Jesus." And, on occasion, Jim would preach with an interpreter at his side. At the end of their first year, they had seen God work in a mighty way and bring three thousand new converts into the kingdom of God.

"The people were so open to the things of God," Marion said.

But not everyone was enthusiastic about the Zirkles' work in spreading the good news of salvation.

"It seems we were always one step ahead of trouble," Marion said, referring to several close calls. "We've been held at gunpoint before. Jim's been searched many times. In fact, my husband received two or three [death] threats. They said if we didn't leave the country, they [communist guerrillas] would kill us."

Still, the Zirkles pressed on, obeying the call that God had given them.

In 1981 they began Living Water Bible School and graduated nineteen students that first year.

"That was our vision," Marion explained, "to teach the nationals all that we had learned about God at Rhema."

The second year their enrollment doubled, and the third year it tripled. Living Water thrived in the midst of war and upheaval. They awoke to gunfire almost every morning for twelve years, but the Zirkles didn't let it shake their faith. They continued to teach the students and train them in evangelism so that they could go out and spread the gospel throughout Guatemala.

"Jim always said that we were safer in Guatemala in God's will than in the United States out of God's will," she said. "Sure, there were times we were scared, but we knew we were right where God wanted us."

Besides, the Zirkles were far too busy to dwell on death threats and gunfire. God was growing Living Water Teaching at an accelerated pace. Building after building went up—dorms, apartments, bungalows, a medical clinic, an orphanage, a dining hall, a school, a church, maintenance buildings, a prayer chapel—more than thirty buildings by 1998. And their Bible school grew, too, adding extension schools in Costa Rica, Honduras, Nicaragua, El Salvador, Panama, Mexico, Paraguay, Japan, Germany, and Sierra Leone. By 1998 Living Water Teaching had graduated more than fifteen thousand students.

The Word of God had taken root in the Guatemalan soil, and Marion and Jim continued in expanding the work as God directed them each step of the way.

TRUSTING GOD IN TRAGEDY

It was Sunday, November 1, 1998—the eleventh anniversary of Living Water Teaching Church—and Marion and Jim were excited to celebrate this special occasion. That's why it seemed odd that Jim wasn't present for the morning service.

Where is he? Marion thought as the service ended.

Jim, their son Jimmy, their son-in-law Chris, their copilot Tom, and right-hand man Raul were all missing. Marion figured they must've been detained by the gloomy weather that Hurricane Mitch had dumped on Guatemala.

Living the LOVE Chapter

The Living Water Teaching team and dozens of volunteers from the States were finishing up a biannual medical campaign, taking the Word of God and medical supplies and treatment to a neighboring city.

At about 3 P.M., Marion walked over to her daughter-in-law's house to see if she had heard from the guys.

"Yes," Laura answered. "Raul called about 1 P.M. to see how the weather was here."

"I thought they'd be back by now," Marion said, giving one of her grandchildren a big bear hug.

Marion stayed at Laura's house, playing with her grandchildren and enjoying the afternoon, when the phone rang.

It's probably them, reporting in, Marion thought.

"Oh, Lord, no!" Laura screamed from the other room.

"What?" Marion shouted.

"The plane has crashed."

"No," Marion said, "don't tell me that."

"It's okay, though," Laura said, still holding the receiver. "They are all alive. They are all walking around."

Naturally, they wanted to get to their loved ones immediately, so Laura left the children with a baby-sitter, and the two of them hopped in Marion's car with two other people and sped off for the small airport.

When they finally got to the airport, they were anxious to find their loved ones, but the plane wasn't there.

Marion began calling out to people in Spanish, "Have you heard anything about a plane crash?" Several people pointed in the direction of a nearby city. So they jumped back into the car and headed that way, racing down the muddy roads. When they arrived at the

Chapter Fifteen — Love Never Fails

small city, they were directed to the top of a steep hill. That's where the plane had gone down—about three kilometers from the airport.

The heavy rains had created so much mud that Marion's car couldn't make it up the hill. They would have to walk. Desperate to reach their loved ones, Marion and Laura trudged through the thick, dark mud, slipping and sliding all the way. Marion struggled up the hill, assisted by a guard who worked for the ministry, as Laura pressed on behind them.

"It was a nightmare," Marion said. "Somewhere along the way, I lost Laura."

When Marion was almost to the top of the hill, a man told her, "There are a lot of dead bodies up there."

"I don't want to hear that!" Marion said sternly. "Don't say any more!"

Covered in mud, Marion finally reached the top of the hill. Fear tried to grip her heart at what she saw before her. The plane was in pieces. It had landed upside down.

"They . . . they told us they were alive," she whispered.

Military and police personnel were milling around everywhere. The whole crash site was chaotic. Marion told one of the police officers, "Look, you are going to let me on the plane."

By this time Marion was in shock, operating on pure adrenaline. She walked onto the ravaged plane, almost afraid to breathe. As she stepped through the debris, the first thing she saw was her husband's resident passport. It was lying next to some of the bodies. She knelt down and picked it up, quickly tucking it into her purse. Next, she found Raul. She touched him and called his name over and over again, but there was no response. He had gone home to be with Jesus.

Panicked, Marion looked at the face of each body that lay nearby, crying over each one. Still, Jim, Jimmy, Chris, and Tom were nowhere inside the plane. Marion breathed a sigh of relief.

They survived, she thought.

Just then, someone called to her, "There are other bodies out in front of the plane."

Marion stepped that direction and saw one body. She asked the person with her to lift up the covering so that she could see who it was.

It was Chris, her son-in-law. Marion wept, feeling so badly for her daughter Kimberly.

"There are three more bodies over here," called one of the pastors.

"Please," Marion begged, "can you see if they are Jim, Jimmy, or Tom?"

The bodies were covered in mud so he couldn't recognize them, but he found a shoe. He held it up. It was Tom's. Marion recognized it.

"They have taken some of the survivors to the general hospital," a policeman informed her.

Marion was sure that Jim and Jimmy would be there.

The sun was setting as Marion headed to the hospital. She was tired, afraid, hurting, and longing to hold her husband and son. When she arrived at the ER, she found five of the seven survivors. She spoke with each one, asking about her husband and son. None of them knew any details. She sat in the waiting room for a long time, hoping to hear some news. Finally, a doctor who attended their church stopped by, and Marion asked him to find out about Jim and Jimmy.

"Please!" she pleaded. "I have to know if they're still alive."

Chapter Fifteen ~ Love Never Fails

"Yes, I will try to find out where they are," he promised her.

Not long after, the doctor returned for Marion. He escorted her to a private hospital, closer to the campus of Living Water Teaching. Marion expected to see Jim and Jimmy when she got there.

"Where are they? I need to see them," Marion said.

"I'm sorry," the doctor said, "but they didn't make it."

"Neither one?" Marion cried out, her body shaking.

"No."

She sat back down, trying to comprehend what she'd just been told. She had heard the news with her ears, but the information hadn't yet made it to her heart. Feeling almost paralyzed, Marion closed her eyes, hoping it was all a bad dream that would go away.

How could I have lost them all? she thought. *How can this be possible?*

She buried her face in her hands, sobbing uncontrollably.

"Let's take you home," the doctor said.

The doctor and his wife and another missionary helped Marion outside and into their car.

Marion walked through the door of the home that she and Jim had shared for so many years. Everything looked the same, but Marion knew it would never be the same again. Her life would never be the same again. Suddenly, she didn't want to be there, so she headed straight for Laura's house.

"I just wanted to hold my grandbabies," Marion remembered.

Overwhelmed by the grief that consumed her, she hugged her little granddaughter for a very long time.

"What happened to you?" Marion asked Laura. "I lost you."

"I never made it to the accident scene," Laura said, pausing. "I just knew Jimmy hadn't made it."

Late that evening, Marion returned to her home and called

Kimberly and her other daughter Debbie, who were both living in Caddo Mills, Texas. They had already been informed about the tragedy, but they needed to talk to their mom.

"We were all devastated," Marion confided. "We just couldn't believe it had happened."

Eighteen had been on the airplane, and only seven had survived. The weather had been sunny when they departed, but it was foggy and rainy when they tried to land. After several attempts to find an opening to land on their grassy runway, the crew decided it was too risky and headed to Guatemala City to land there. Unfortunately, the visibility wasn't any better at that location, so they circled back to their airport, looking for a hole in the cloud cover. Finally, they found one and tried to land the plane, but they didn't come down over the landing strip. Instead, the DC-3 hit a tree and broke off its left wing, flipping the plane upside down. Those in the front of the plane were killed.

CARRYING ON THE LOVE

After the first few funerals on Monday, Marion asked all the missionaries to come to her home. Though her heart was broken with grief, she had prayed much during the last few days. And she had made a decision.

"I am going on," she told them through tears. "This is God's ministry, and the devil is not going to win. Their deaths are not going to be in vain!"

Determination filled every ounce of Marion's body. That night after she'd met with her staff, Marion retreated to her bathroom and screamed, "Devil, you're not going to win. We are going to win more souls than ever before."

Chapter Fifteen ~ Love Never Fails

And that's what they've done.

Since the accident almost three years ago, much has been accomplished for the Lord. Today, more than 45 percent of Guatemala's population is Christian, and Living Water Teaching Bible School has graduated more than seventeen thousand students from its Guatemalan and extension schools. Marion is still running with the vision.

"I have been tempted to throw in the towel a few times, but God has kept us here," she said. "If it wasn't for God and His love, and the prayers of the body of Christ, I would not have made it. Whenever I felt as though I was going to fail, God would pour His love into me. I could feel His arms around me. I could feel Him saying, 'I love you. You can do it.' He never left me—not one time. I can honestly say that today we are in victory!"

Of course, Marion still aches for Jim—her husband, best friend, and spiritual leader—and for her son and son-in-law and the others who had died in the plane crash. But carrying out the vision that they all so strongly believed in somehow makes the pain more bearable.

"Jesus heals. My heart has healed a lot in three years," she said. "I can look at their picture now without crying, so that's progress."

And God has healed Kimberly's and Laura's hearts, too. Both have remarried since the accident and continue working with Living Water Teaching.

"We don't live in grief every day," Marion shared. "We live in victory. That's how Jim would've wanted it. He was such a visionary. We walked together in the vision, and because of what he put in us, we are able to continue on with the work God called us to in Guatemala."

Today, a memorial garden stands on campus as a reminder of the lives that were lost and the love that goes on.

"You could not go through something like this without Jesus," Marion said. "Now, more than ever, I can say that God's love never fails. It has never failed me."

When tragedy strikes, many people blame God. Certainly, Marion Zirkle could have gone down that road. She could have said, "But, God! Jim, Jimmy, Chris, Tom, Raul—they were all serving you! How could you let this happen?" But Marion didn't ask those accusatory questions. Instead of blaming God, she turned to God, relying on His love to get her through each minute, each month, each year.

Maybe you're going through a time of grief, and you don't know if you can carry the pain another day. Maybe you've endured many storms in life and feel as if God has abandoned you. Well, He hasn't. Just as Marion has experienced, God never leaves us nor forsakes us—that's a promise from His Word.

God loves you. The Father wants you to crawl up in His lap so He can comfort you today. He hurts when you hurt. He wants to see you through this time of tragedy. He wants to see you come out victorious on the other side. The key is this—don't blame God. Instead, allow Him to love you and heal you. His love never fails—just ask Marion.

FOR FURTHER STUDY: Read Joel 3:10; 1 John 4:16-17; Colossians 2:2; Ephesians 4:15; Ephesians 5:2.

APPENDIX A
Prayer for Salvation

Heavenly Father, it is written in your Word that if I confess with my mouth that Jesus is Lord and believe in my heart that you have raised Him from the dead, that I shall be saved. So, Father, I do that right now, in Jesus' Name. I turn away from my old life, and I look forward to a new life with you.

I thank you, Father, for forgiving my sins and cleansing me from all unrighteousness. I praise you, Lord, that I am a new creature in Christ Jesus. Help me today to begin living the Love Chapter in my life. In Jesus' Mighty Name. Amen.